BRISTOL FRENCH POETRY GROUP

INTRODUCTION
TO
FRENCH POETRY

Editorial matter © Department of French, University of Bristol, 1983

Acknowledgements

We are grateful to holders of copyright for permission to reproduce poems as follows:

Editions Gallimard: Poems IV, Vb, VIb, 57, 58, 59, 63, 64, 65,
                               66, 69, 70, 72, 73, 74, 75, 76, 77

M. Louis Aragon: Poems 67, 68

Editions Le Terrain Vague: Poem 71

Librairie José Corti: Poem 78

M. Léo Ferré: Poem 79

Editions Musicales 57:   Poem 80

Mercure de France: Poem 81

Editions du Seuil: Poem 82

Société Nationale d'Edition et de Diffusion,
Alger: Poem 83

First published 1983

Reprinted with corrections 1987, 1988, 1998

PREFACE

The overall plan of this volume, and the choice of poems, are the fruit of discussions between all six contributors; individual sections of the introduction, however, and the specimen commentaries, reflect the viewpoint of individuals, although we have each benefited from the comments and criticisms of our colleagues. We hope that the differences in approach and emphasis will enlighten rather than confuse the reader.

In common with many other teachers of poetry, we feel that comparisons between poems can be fruitful in helping students to see what is distinctive in each individual poem. We have therefore included two double commentaries, which may serve to illustrate this approach, and in choosing the poems for the second half of the volume we have aimed at providing scope for further comparisons. In order to avoid imposing any particular comparisons by a thematic grouping, we have presented the poems in the conventional chronological order, with possible links indicated in footnotes; this arrangement will, we hope, provide the maximum flexibility, allowing for comparisons to be made on the basis of form, structure or tone, as well as subject matter. Such comparisons are, of course, an optional extra, which may be utilised or ignored according to individual preference; the poems we have chosen are all, we believe, worthy of study in their own right. We would emphasise, however, that although our selection includes some familiar anthology pieces, it is not intended to provide a historical survey of the best poems in French, or even of representative poems by the most important poets (the selection would certainly have been different if that had been our aim); it is a collection of poems through which students may develop their critical faculties in relation to French poetry.

Annotations to the poems have been kept to a minimum; we have assumed that students will have access to standard dictionaries and works of reference, and will use them.

J. M. Dixon
P. G. Hawkins
T. D. Hemming
M. J. O'Regan
S. W. Taylor
S. A. Warman

CONTENTS

1. The Challenge of French Poetry

Poetry is for most of us the first literary genre that we meet; even before story-telling, rhymes rock baby to sleep or accompany a bounce up and down on mother's knee. The primary patterns and rhythms of verse in our native language are assimilated with the language itself. Even the mature, sophisticated products of the major poets in the language may retain beneath their elaboration echoes and elements of the simplest and most basic devices of rhyme and rhythm that were among the first things our ears took in. The absence in a foreign language and literature of these familiar features may well constitute a barrier to appreciation that should not be under-estimated, for poetry (or at any rate lyric poetry) is not only the first literary genre that we encounter; it is also the one which is, of its very nature, meant to speak most directly to the emotions. A poem, to be successful, is likely to demand of the reader or listener a subjective response in which the role of reason may well be very slight. In our own language we may find ourselves enticed into a poem; an interest and a response may be sparked off at first, by some recognisably familiar pattern of rhyme or rhythm, reproduced or perhaps, as with some modern poets, teasingly distorted and varied.

French verse at the formal level is on the face of it sufficiently similar to English verse – using rhyme and metre – for us perhaps to anticipate the pleasure of familiarity. But the similarities are deceptive; the metrical and rhyming conventions prove to be so different that our expectations, if they have ever been aroused, may be quickly frustrated. Metre may prove a disappointment, for to an English ear there may seem to be no beat, no regularity, no true rhythm such as we are used to. Rhyming conventions likewise include cases that English has never readily accepted, such as identical rhyme (*plante* (noun) and *plante* (verb) rhyme in French) and disyllabic or even polysyllabic rhyme which is typically and mainly reserved in English for light and comic verse. Irregularity is an essential feature of English prosody; that there is from Marot, or at least Malherbe, to Mallarmé no such thing as an irregular alexandrine, nor any departure from the rule that masculine and feminine rhymes must alternate, may suggest an oppressive, inflexible rigidity of formal convention.

The problems in respect of form are paralleled at the level of poetic diction and style. Although at most periods there are quite close similarities in the subject-matter of poetry in both languages, the treatment of the themes is often very different. At least until the twentieth century, the main problem in respect of poetic diction is that,

i

generally, French poets have seemed far more rhetorical. Many French poets seem to have been drawn, even in poems on perennial lyric themes, towards what may strike us as a somewhat magniloquent, oratorical style, making much use of devices such as antithesis and anaphora, often building up to grand climaxes. If the English tradition offers stylistic parallels, they are mainly in the realm of public poetry; in general, a quieter voice has been felt more suitable for the expression of the typically intimate themes of personal lyricism. The distinction between public and private poetry is less clearly marked in the French tradition, and again the temptation is there for the English reader: it is difficult to escape from the feeling that what we are used to is right.

It follows from what I have been saying so far that there is a fundamental challenge to the English reader's appreciation of French poetry. Is it in fact possible to acquire, to learn, what in our own language is rooted in experience? Some people seem to hold with emotional tenacity the position that poetry is worthwhile and meaningful only if it inspires an instantaneous response, a gut reaction. This attitude would effectively preclude the *study* of poetry in any language, including one's own, and the mature products of major poets (which are hardly likely to yield up all their secrets on the first, or even the fiftieth reading) would be the principal victims. It cannot be seriously argued, though it may be passionately asserted, that the proper criterion for judging a work of literature is the reader's immediate reaction. If literature is worth studying, as distinct from being something from which any individualistic response is permissible, and all such responses, however gratuitous, capricious or arbitrary, are equally valid – or invalid – then there is a clear need for some agreed criteria. These should naturally be, as far as possible, objective, in the sense that they should be independent of personal caprice; they should also be appropriate. However natural it may be for us, we must avoid falling into the trap of applying to French poetry norms appropriate to English poetry.

Poetry in a foreign language must of necessity be an acquired taste; all the contributors to this volume firmly believe that it is possible to acquire the taste, and well worth doing, but we do not share the view (found in some well-known manuals) that failure to recognise intuitively and respond fully and instantly to the subtle charms of French poetry is the mark of a blunted sensibility or a jaded palate.

Having in mind the various possible obstacles, we may suggest some possible ways in which the English reader may find his bearings. The unfamiliarity of the formal conventions of poetry, for example, is only one facet of the whole challenge of attempting to learn a foreign language. Unless the chance of long residence or the advantage of parentage has enabled us to become genuinely bilingual, we are not likely to possess the complete linguistic mastery of the native speaker. The acquisition of the true sense of the poetic characteristics and resources of the language is a vital aspect of the proper knowledge of the language as a whole. Contact with poetry can and should develop and enhance our sensitivity to and awareness of rhythms and sonorities – in a broad sense, the aesthetic resources and characteristics of the language – as well as developing our awareness of nuances of meaning and association. In this way poetry increases and enhances our real command and grasp of the language that we are trying to master; but at the same time, as our grasp of the language develops, so will our responsiveness to its poetry.

We also need to recognise that, at a more strictly stylistic level, all poetry, indeed all literature, involves convention. It may therefore be sensible to make our first approaches to French poetry *via* poems and poets where the weight of convention is (or appears to be) less heavy, or where the conventions themselves seem more familiar. The sort of French verse for which we may well find it easiest to acquire a taste to begin with is likely to be the sort where we encounter the fewest alien (and therefore potentially off-putting) conventions and tricks. Conspicuously among literary genres poetry benefits from a non-chronological approach; and in practice this leads us to modern poetry. By no means all contemporary French poets are obscure or difficult to understand. Notably there are the song-writers, such as Brassens and Léo Ferré, unquestionable poets who at the same time are direct in their means of expression, and who enjoy very wide popular appeal. As well as these, there are many poets, not themselves musicians, whose words have been set to music in a popular idiom and have won wide acclaim. The name of Prévert immediately comes to mind. But *non-chronological* does not only mean *modern*. Like Prévert, François Villon, who lived in the middle of the fifteenth century, has been set to music by modern performers, and is certainly regarded by the public as a *poète d'aujourd'hui*. He has for the modern sensibility an immediacy that many other poets of past centuries perhaps lack. He is in fact an instructive and revealing test case. No doubt the reason for his contemporary appeal is the immediate impact of his anguished lyricism. Yet if we look at him not just in terms of what he has to say, but also in respect of his form, we discover a technical virtuoso, a master of a poetic discipline of extreme rigour, able to handle a set of poetic conventions so strict that the untutored reader might suppose them to be impossibly inhibiting and the negation of poetic inspiration. Villon embodies to perfection the paradoxical strength of the French poetic tradition, namely that seemingly burdensome, indeed, from one point of view, absurd formal restraints and rules have in the event been a stimulus to poetic achievement. It is precisely the exploration of this interaction between individual inspiration and formal constraint that constitutes the fascination of the study of French poetry. Between *form* and *content*, between the *rules* and the poet's imagination and invention, a tension is set up which is the source of the poem's impact. The French poetic tradition offers few instances of the illusion (for it is always an illusion) of the *spontaneous overflow of powerful feeling*. It offers many of the containment of emotion within a form; which is one definition of art, and not perhaps the worst.

T.D.H.

2. The Technique of Commentary

The aims of commentary are two-fold: firstly to deepen and enrich one's appreciation of the poem by observant reading, and secondly to formulate and record or communicate this appreciation. In the first place, therefore, a successful commentary requires a close attention to the observable *facts*, the pattern of sounds, words and meanings of which the poem is composed, and an ability to react to it intellectually, imaginatively or emotively; secondly, it requires powers of lucid expression, so that the links between the text and the reader's reaction to it may be clearly seen. In the initial stage, some kind of balance must be maintained between objective study and subjective reaction, although the exact 'point of balance' will vary from poem to poem; a purely *objective* commentary may be a masterpiece as a technical exercise, but will remain an arid piece of work, whilst a purely *subjective* commentary will often fail to convince, as subjective reactions to a poem may vary considerably: the reader of your commentary may not be disposed to accept your reaction to the poem in preference to his own unless you present the evidence on which it is based. In a complex poem, many different factors have to be observed and weighed up, and the emphasis given to each is a matter of personal judgement. It does not follow, however, that all personal judgements are equally valid: an assessment that totally ignores certain aspects of a poem while over-emphasising others may meet with a hostile reception, especially if it is the result of approaching the poem with too many rigid preconceptions about the author and the kind of poetry he wrote. But the extent to which a poem limits possible responses is immensely variable: some poems work within a narrow framework of predictable responses, where the reader is shepherded from one emotional reaction to another, in others deliberate imprecision of expression gives the reader almost unlimited freedom.

As students of poetry written in a foreign language, it is all too easy for us to misinterpret a French poem at the most basic level, through actual mistranslation, or through a failure to appreciate the connotations (as opposed to the literal meaning) that certain words or images have in French. Completely unfamiliar words are not a serious problem: we simply look them up in a dictionary (but a dictionary, of course, which gives sufficient examples for us to get some idea of the contexts in which the word is used, and the connotations it may have). The apparently familiar words are a more insidious problem, to which there is no simple answer, except to beware of jumping to conclusions. For example, one translates the two words *dormir avec* as *sleep with*, and it is all too easy to assume that the French phrase has the same sexual connotations as the English; but a moment's thought (or again, a check in the dictionary) shows that *dormir* always implies inactivity, and that the French equivalent of *sleep with* in the sexual sense is *coucher avec*. So the first priority is to *understand* the poem on a basic level: a subtle and elaborate account of patterns of imagery collapses like a card house if it is founded on a misapprehension.

Once this initial stage has been completed, the critical appreciation of the poem can begin. From this point onwards, we need to hold in our hand two threads, the one being the objective observation of what is in the poem, the other our own subjective reactions to it. At every stage we must inter-relate these two threads: every time we observe an element in the text of the poem, we should ask ourselves 'So what?' (or, more politely, 'What is the effect of this?'), and every time we react subjectively, we should ask, 'What has produced this effect?'. If we maintain this constant to-ing and fro-ing, we should be able to avoid the dangers of futile objectivity ("The poem contains 23 adjectives, and alliteration is used in lines 13 and 17") and of effusive subjectivity ("The poem conveys a sense of peace and tranquillity") – the sort of conclusion that will only convince if it is supported by detailed analysis.

With few exceptions a poem, like other forms of linguistic communication, makes its impression in a 'linear' way: the words, and thus the ideas and images, are presented in a fixed order, and we expect to start at the beginning and work through to the end. In this respect a poem is quite unlike a painting, which we see all at once, even though we may be encouraged to 'read' it by looking successively at different areas. The poet may modify the linear progression by the use of repetition, so that we appear to move in a circle, or a succession of circles, coming back to the same point, but it remains true that the majority of poems do have a linear 'thread' or 'development'; poems where phrases, lines or stanzas can be rearranged at random are very rare, even in the experimental twentieth century. The stages in which this development take place form the inner 'structure' of the poem; it may take the form of a clearly marked 'argument' (a logical progression of ideas), a narrative (a sequence of events), or a sequence of images, grouped around one or more themes or developing one from another in a kind of chain. It may harmonise closely with elements of external structure (versification, stanza forms), as when each stanza of a poem develops a single image or a single, clear-cut stage in the argument; but it is also possible for the inner structure of a poem to cut across the external framework in a kind of counterpoint.

The 'inner structure' of the poem provides the framework within which we can turn an increasingly attentive eye to the details, which we must aim to see always in relation to the poem of which they form a part. It is their function in a context which gives them significance; although it may sometimes be convenient to group together examples of a particular feature in a poem (the use of adjectives, for example), this can only be done when the function of each adjective in its context has been examined. In commentaries that have been polished up for publication, this groundwork may not be clearly visible: the writer may take it for granted that his readers will themselves have done the basic work on the poem concerned, but he too will certainly have done it at some stage in the preparation of his commentary.

Many of the kinds of detail which may be observed in a close study of a poem will already be familiar, so rather than simply enumerating them I would like to suggest ways of handling some of the most important ones. In many poems, *imagery*, in its widest sense, will be one of the most obvious features: what should we look for in a poetic image? Many people would say 'originality' – but there are not very many truly original images, and if that were all that we looked for, we should soon come to the end of our search, without having discovered much about what makes an image work in a poem. More important than originality is the power of suggestion in an image, and this depends not only on the raw material, the words used to express the image, but on the way in which the connotations of these words are enhanced or enriched by the context, or by other images in close proximity.

So in analysing images we must establish both the *potential* connotation of each image, and consider how those connotations are developed or limited by the context. The specimen commentaries show this type of analysis applied to specific situations as part of the study of a complete poem; by looking at a smaller unit (a single stanza), we can perhaps focus more sharply on the kind of questions that need to be asked if we are to succeed in unravelling the often complex interactions between images.

The following lines are the opening stanza of a love poem by Théophile de Viau, published in 1621:

> Quand tu me vois baiser tes bras,
> Que tu poses nus sur les draps,
> Bien plus blancs que le linge même;
> Quand tu sens ma brûlante main
> Se promener dessus ton sein,
> Tu sens bien, Cloris, que je t'aime.

It will be noted that these lines contain little imagery in the technical sense of metaphors and similes (*brûlante* and *se promener* are the only words used metaphorically, and in line 3, relating to a specific object, *le linge*, actually present in the scene, is a comparison rather than a simile); the stanza as a whole nevertheless constitutes a complex image, a web of sense impressions conjured up in the reader's mind.

We might start our analysis by looking at the nouns: *bras, draps, linge, main, sein* all denote concrete objects of which we may form an image in our mind's eye. Of these five nouns, three *(bras, main, sein)* have a wide range of potential connotations, arising from the possible functions of the parts of the body concerned: does the context impose any restrictions on these potential connotations? The answer is clearly 'Yes': for example, the word *bras,* with its two adjectives *nus* and *blancs* (both of which attract some attention through being separated from the noun), has connotations quite different from those it might have when a Cornelian hero speaks, for example, of *les exploits de son bras,* in the sense of 'deeds of valour'. Such examples as this, where the connotations of a word are immediately limited by the general context, may seem too obvious to need mentioning in a commentary, but they should at least be observed as part of the background against which a more precise image is set. In this case the reader's response to the nouns is modified not only by the adjectives *(nus, blancs, brûlante)* which qualify them grammatically, but also by the verbs associated with them. Our first reaction to the images is influenced by the verb *vois*: it appears that we are being invited to concentrate on the visual aspect of the image. But the dependent infinitive *baiser* immediately offsets this with an idea of physical contact, and this emphasis on the sense of touch is maintained by *tu poses, se promener dessus* and the first *tu sens*. The final line of the stanza, now using *tu sens* to denote emotional awareness, fits the images into an intellectual argument: sense-impressions are the source of emotions.

Beneath this broad structure, however, there is another layer of meaning which can be detected by taking a closer look at the adjective *blancs,* one of the recurrent 'key-words' in poetry, because of its exceptionally wide range of potential connotations. Its immediate context (the comparison of *bien plus blancs que linge même*), and the verb *vois* seem to underline its literal, visual meaning, but the link with *baiser tes bras* is sufficient to keep alive some of its abstract connotations (innocence, purity, virginity), and the comparison with *linge,* though superficially restricted to the sense of sight, also conjures up an impression of coolness. These half-hidden suggestions are brought to the surface by *brûlante*: the idea of passion in *brûlante* emphasises, by contrast, the latent ideas of virginity and coolness, frigidity even, in *blancs,* and conversely we become more aware of the red colour implied by *brûlante*. The interaction between *blancs* and *brûlante* thus stresses some of the connotations of each, so that from two simple and, at first sight, conventional adjectives we obtain a relatively complex impression of a contrast between white and red, cold and hot, passive feminine purity and active masculine passion.

No two poems pose identical problems; in some cases, as in the stanza we have just examined, links and contrasts between images may limit or develop certain aspects of their connotations in a relatively clear structure, which nevertheless leaves some scope for different individual reactions. (Each reader's reaction to the idea of whiteness, for example, depends on the sum of his past experience; although for the most part this is conditioned by cultural background, normally shared by the poet and his contemporary public, there will always be some differences between individual readers). In other cases, however, particularly in the poetry of the last hundred years or so, the poet will not give us such clear signposts, and we must resist the temptation to impose our own pattern. Verlaine expressed a preference for

la chanson grise/Où l'Indécis au Précis se joint:

it is our role as readers and students of poetry to illuminate the ambiguities and uncertainties, but not to give precision to what is intentionally blurred. In many cases, the poet will have used *his* imagination to encourage us to use *ours*; whereas some poetry can be shown to have a *logical* structure, leading us through a certain sequence of mental acts, others simply encourage us to think *about* certain things, without imposing a rigid pattern of relationships between them. In Eluard's *La terre est bleue comme une orange*, for example, the explicit rejection of our 'normal' view of the world forces us to take a fresh look at each of the three components of the image, and to experiment with possible relationships between them. As in the stanza analysed above, the prime necessity in coming to terms with the image is an awareness of the potential connotations of the words; but in the case of Eluard's poem the assessment of the overall impact of the image depends more on imagination and correspondingly less on rational analysis.

In the preceding paragraphs I have used the word 'image' loosely to refer to any word that triggers off some kind of response in the reader's imagination, or to the response itself. It should be apparent that this 'image-forming' function in a poem is not confined to words that are used 'figuratively', in metaphors or similes; virtually any word, even when apparently used literally, has connotations which the writer may use to slant or enrich his surface 'meaning'. Rhetoric and propaganda make use of the emotive connotations of words to win support for a particular viewpoint; poetry more often uses them to build up a texture of meaning that is denser and more complex than that of ordinary prose. The very fact that a piece of writing is presented as a poem creates certain expectations in the reader as to the way it uses language – more so in French where the tradition of a 'literary language' has always been stronger than in English. As a result, poetry can achieve forceful effects by the use of language that is unexpected in its context, as well as through the original combinations of words that are the most obvious linguistic expression of the poet's creativity. This type of contrast is most clearly seen in the work of writers such as Rimbaud, who seek to shock their readers into a new vision of the world by setting the conventional moral abstractions of poetic diction beside the mundane objects of the material world; the device is used in a more sophisticated way in Francis Ponge's *La Bougie* (poem no.69), where the technical term *pédoncule* joins with the matter-of-fact syntax to create an impression of scientific precision in a description which is otherwise composed almost entirely of metaphors which belong to the traditional diction of poetry.

It should be clear from these notes on the analysis of poetic imagery that the principal task is to establish the connotations of image-forming words, singly and in relation to each other – a task that involves looking not only at the context of each word in the poem under discussion, but also at the kind of contexts in which it is used elsewhere. To do this successfully, we must bring into play the whole breadth of our knowledge of the French language and of French literature, which will direct us towards the associations of words and ideas that might have been present in the author's mind, rather than towards an arbitrary interpretation of our own. In interpreting a poem we should aim to draw out what is in the text, not to create a kind of parallel text prefaced by the words 'The poem means that'. The poet has, after all, chosen to write a poem, and although it would be futile to speculate on the precise reasons for his choice, we can at least be sure that, to some extent, the 'medium' does affect the 'message', and that the 'meaning' of a poem can never be conveyed adequately in any different form.

At the same time as we 'interpret' the images of a poem we should observe the verbal forms in which they are expressed: it is, after all, through words that poetic images are transmitted from poet to reader. External features of form make an immediate visual impact: it will be obvious whether the poem is in stanzas, in continuous verse, or in irregular sections, or indeed whether it is in verse at all. If it is in verse, any variations in the length of lines used, whether irregular or in a fixed pattern, will be apparent, and indeed you will often have a pretty shrewd idea of the length of the lines before you think about counting the syllables. Some readers prefer not to pay close attention to the formal and metrical aspects of the poem until they have observed all they can on the level of 'meaning': but there are arguments in favour of looking at the formal characteristics at an early stage, as this formal pattern, and more especially variations within it, may have a fundamental contribution to make. The details of metrical analysis are dealt with elsewhere, but a word may be added at this point on an aspect of the relationship between 'external' and 'internal' structure that comes between the detailed analysis of the lines and the more general study of the poem as a whole: that is, the correlation between verse-forms and stanza-forms and the development of the theme of the poem. The traditional poetic forms are patterns imposed on the development of ideas: once a poet has decided, for example, to write a sonnet in alexandrines, he is no longer a free agent in what he writes, but must conform to the restrictions which that first decision entails. The degree of conflict or tension which arises between form and content is of course infinitely varied: in some poems, the 'internal' and 'external' structures may coincide exactly, in that perfect harmony of form and content that is the ideal of classical theories of poetry, but in many poems, the external structure provides a much looser kind of framework. Just as it is important in studying versification to be aware of *enjambement* between lines, it is important to observe the unity or otherwise of the larger metrical unit, the stanza. Is the poem composed of a series of independent units, in which each *metrical* unit (stanza) consists of a single *sense* unit (sentence), or do the sentences appear to develop at cross-purposes with the stanzas, spilling over from stanza to stanza or stopping abruptly half-way through? The answers to these questions may explain a good deal about the overall feelings of tension, dynamism or repose that emerge from a poem written in stanzas.

In addition to the *regular* patterns of external structure, which appeal most obviously to the human desire for recognisably repeated patterns as a means of making sense of the diversity of experience, many poems make use of less rigorous patterns of sound or structure, which may be treated under the general heading of 'pattern rhetoric'. The effects of these flexible patterns, which are not predetermined by the poet's initial choice of verse form, are many and varied: they may create an atmosphere of formality, simply because they *are* patterns, but they may also enhance an emotional atmosphere, or suggest relationships between words – emphasising relationships already established by the syntax, in many cases, but sometimes running counter to the syntax, and suggesting relationships that the syntax, the logical, grammatical connection between words, either omits or explicitly excludes. For example, Paul Eluard's poem *Pour vivre ici* includes in a sequence of images the line:

Les nids et leurs oiseaux, les maisons et leurs clés:

a pattern is established in which we would expect the final word to be, perhaps, *habitants*, standing in the same relationship to *maisons* as *oiseaux* does to *nids*. We end up with a double image, in which the image that is actually present in the text, *clés*, is superimposed on the image that is suggested by the pattern, *habitants*.

The most obvious forms of pattern rhetoric are repetition and contrast; *variation* involves a combination of the two, with an underlying metrical or syntactic structure being repeated, while one or more of its constituent elements is changed. Repetitions of words are usually easy to observe and assess, in that they establish the repeated word as conveying a dominant idea; similarly, contrasts between words with opposing meanings or connotations (antithesis) may give extra force to an argument. At first sight repetitions of syntactic or metrical patterns are likely to have a more purely aesthetic effect, being pleasing in themselves; but as ideas expressed in a recognisable pattern tend to anchor themselves more firmly in the memory (an important aspect of oral poetry), repetitions and variations of this kind may also be a way of underlining and enhancing the literal 'meaning' of an expression. For example, Baudelaire's line

La langoureuse Asie et la brûlante Afrique

gains its evocative power from the parallelism of the construction as well as from the choice and positioning of the adjectives.

The line just quoted introduces the most difficult to handle (though perhaps the most familiar) of all the various forms of pattern: patterns of sound. Whereas repetition of words or structures in close proximity is virtually certain to be deliberate, and therefore significant, repetition of sounds may more easily occur through pure coincidence; on the other hand both writers and readers of poetry are likely to be more sensitive to sound than writers or readers of prose, so that echoes that are apparently trivial and insignificant may make a contribution to the overall impact of the poem. But if in *theory* the distinction between 'accidental' and 'significant' repetitions of sounds may shrink to vanishing point, for practical purposes we need to separate the occasional repetitions of individual sounds from the more obvious patterns of alliteration and assonance that may constitute a vital ingredient in the emotive or imaginative force of a poem. We should be able to recognise significant sound-patterns by following our two threads of cause and effect: if a sound-pattern is significant, it will produce a recognisable effect in heightening or enriching the implications of the words in which it occurs; conversely, if a line or stanza produces a sense of harmony or musicality, it should be possible to pin down the sources of that impression.

The approach to sound-patterns is one of the greatest sources of disagreement between readers of poetry, because subjective responses must inevitably play a vital role; but sound-patterns are too important for us to ignore them simply because it is impossible to achieve a consensus. I would suggest as a guiding principle that the inevitable subjectivity of reactions to sound-patterns should be accepted, but dealt with in a rational way: if you feel that your appreciation of the poem is enhanced by patterns of sound, and if you think you can explain these patterns and communicate your reactions to your readers, then your comments will be worth reading; but if the sound-patterns in a given poem 'do nothing for you', it is better not to mention them than to invent a significance for them. There are three basic situations in which sound-patterns may be significant:

(1) If the sound of the words echoes their sense (see Onomatopoeia in the Glossary);

(2) If they underline a relationship between words of focal importance;

(3) If there is a build up of identical or closely related sounds that goes beyond what might happen accidentally.

If the second criterion is satisfied, the alliteration or assonance may be extremely effective without being very extensive, as for example, in the line from Baudelaire quoted above, where the syllable [lã] occuring in *langoureuse* and *brûlante*, helps to draw together the two adjectives which are parallel and yet contrasted. Here, as in a great many cases, sound-patterns work in conjunction with patterns of syntax and rhythm to produce a cumulative effect that is far greater than could be produced by any of these elements on its own. More extensive alliterations are not necessarily more effective: they may in fact have less poetic value, in that they may draw attention to themselves as specimens of technical virtuosity, rather than unobtrusively enhancing the suggestive power of the poem.

Having read the poem as carefully and thoroughly as possible, we now have to present our observations and reactions in an orderly manner. Our reading of the poem is valid for *us*: will it be acceptable to others? A commentary on a poem is in many ways more difficult to organise than a commentary on an extract from a play or novel, where there are certain obvious questions, such as context, character and plot, but many of the more general *do's* and *don't's* of commentary apply to poetry as to other genres. The first and most important principle is to allow the poem to speak for itself, as a unique work of art, and not to treat it from the beginning as an *example*, illustrating preconceptions about its author or the period in which it was written. (Commentaries of that type may have a part to play in literary or cultural history, but they have no place in literary *criticism*, which is what this book is about). A commentary that starts off with sweeping generalisations will not *necessarily* lead to a distorted reading of the poem, but it may very well give the impression that the poem is being pushed willy-nilly into a framework determined in advance.

Because most poems are virtually self-contained entities, the question of context, which is the traditional starting point for most other commentaries, is often irrelevant; if the poem can be understood on its own, it is usually best to postpone consideration of its relationship to the rest of the author's work until the end of the commentary, where some broadening of scope is appropriate.

As to the vexed question of subdivisions within the commentary, we have to decide, either as a matter of general principle or as a question to be asked afresh every time we compose a formal commentary, whether it is better to divide it up into separate sections on theme, development, form and style or to treat the whole exercise as a single unit. My own view is that there is a good deal to be said for starting with a brief analysis of the development of the theme (the 'internal structure'), and the form of verse and stanzas used (the 'external structure'); it is much easier to present the details of the poem if the general framework has been explained at the outset. The inherent danger of this form of presentation is that the structural analysis may degenerate into mere paraphrase, a résumé of 'what the poet says', which leaves us no wiser as to the organisation of the material. But paraphrase is a pitfall which should be avoidable if we have a clear idea of what we are trying to do.

Once the stage has been set, the detailed examination can begin. It will no doubt be clear by this stage that I firmly believe that much, if not all, of the point of close reading of a poem is lost if an attempt is made to separate form and content; I believe that this is also true when it comes to putting our assessment into the shape of a commentary. Poetry is a form of communication that depends to a large extent on a subtle balancing of the connotations of individual words; it is extremely difficult to analyse the *content* of a poem satisfactorily without alluding to the *choice* and arrangement of words, and even more difficult to talk about *style* as if it could exist independently. This is not to say that you will not come across competent, or even excellent commentaries in which this division is adopted; but in my view it entails too great a risk of underestimating the *interaction* between words, thoughts and feelings to be used unless you are very sure of your ground. I would advise presenting your reading of the poem in much the same form as you originally showed the links between the objectively observable features of the poem and your reactions to it.

As in all writing on literary topics, you should ensure that your statements have evidence to support them; but this does not mean quoting and transcribing from the poem at every turn. It is assumed that the reader of your commentary has the text of your poem in front of him, so there is no point in telling him: 'The poet says . . .' and then quoting at length. You will need to refer to individual words, phrases, images and so on, and in that case, direct quotation of the poet's words is obviously necessary; if you wish to refer to a longer passage, then line or stanza numbers are usually sufficient. (Note that in dealing with French poetry it is customary, and desirable in order to avoid ambiguity, to use the term 'stanza' for groups of lines conforming to a regular pattern; 'verse' leads to a confusion with the French *vers*, which means a 'line'. I find that the safest procedure is to use 'line' and 'stanza' and avoid the word 'verse' altogether, except as a generic term to refer to 'that which is not prose'). The only occasion in a commentary when you may need to quote at any length is when you are dealing with patterns: the clearest way of presenting these is often to transcribe the relevant lines and underline the repeated or contrasting elements. The use of different forms of underlining can enable quite complex information to be conveyed succinctly. This does not, of course, mean that a suitably underlined quotation is all that is needed in these cases; as always, explanation of the significance of your observations is also needed, and this will entail *describing* the patterns, not merely presenting them. Where sound patterns are concerned, make use of your knowledge of phonetics to describe them, and transpose relevant syllables into International Phonetic Symbols; this will not only make your arguments more cogent, but at an earlier stage in the proceedings it will save you from falling into the trap of assuming that repeated letters indicate repeated sounds.

At first sight, the presence of a clearly-defined piece of material may appear to make a commentary on a poem an easier exercise than a more wide-ranging essay on a poet's work; but it can be more demanding, in that it depends to a much greater extent on critical perception, for which mere skill in the accumulation and organisation of material can never be a satisfactory substitute. But how do we learn 'critical perception', or improve on what we already have? There is no short answer, for 'critical perception' is not something that exists in a vacuum, or in a water-tight compartment labelled 'French Poetry'. It is the product of all the experience of life, real as well as cultural. For example, images in a French poem will be significant to you because you have already come across the same or similar images elsewhere in literature or in art, or because they relate to things you have experienced directly; so the idea that commentary on a poem, a text of limited dimensions, is necessarily a limited and limiting exercise is a false one. The greatest poems are a concentration or distillation of a rich experience, and in writing a commentary you are, as it were, unlocking that experience from the verbal text in which it has been preserved. As a student of literature you will be constantly extending your own experience in many different directions, by deliberate study or otherwise; this is the foundation of all literary studies, not only of the study of poetry – for example, when we ask ourselves whether the characters in a play or novel are *convincing*, we are considering the work in terms of our own experience. In our own context, 'critical perception' is the ability to set out the links between the poem as an expression of an aspect of the poet's experience or vision of life and our own experience; it involves the careful and conscious manipulation of those two intertwined threads mentioned earlier, the analysis of the objective facts of the poem and the reactions which they produce in the reader.

The number of formal written commentaries which you may be called upon to produce during your student career may be small, but the technique of commentary outlined here is fundamentally a technique of *reading*, and every time you read a French poem something of the same process will take place in your mind. We hope that the academic exercise of commentary will enrich your sensitivity to poetry, rather than stultify it, and make the reading of poetry a rewarding activity.

S.A.W.

3. Versification

The following notes constitute only a cursory introduction to a very complex subject. Practically every statement made here would be challenged by one or more competent authorities, and in our own century the traditional principles of versification have been very considerably relaxed. The aim, however, is to give an outline, for the benefit of English readers new to the subject, of the basic rules of French versification as they were more or less generally accepted from the seventeenth to the nineteenth centuries. In order to keep the notes brief the only line dealt with is the alexandrine, the line of twelve syllables; it has been the commonest line used in French verse since the end of the sixteenth century, and most of the principles it embodies apply with only the most obvious modifications to lines of other lengths – the commonest of which are the decasyllable and the octosyllable. A second, and deliberate omission is the question of the stanza – *la strophe* in French (the term 'verse', to mean a repeated pattern of line-lengths and rhymes, can lead to confusion and is best avoided). It may however be noted in passing that the stanza is, by French critics, held to require a more intricate rhyme scheme than that of simple *rimes plates* (aa bb, etc). The simplest stanza form consists therefore of four lines of the same length (the isometric stanza) with the rhyme scheme *abab* or *abba*.

The Elements of French Versification

In order of importance these are:

Rhyme
Syllabism
Stress or accentuation.

These elements are more often than not found in English poetry, but in the reverse order of importance, with the 'beat' or stress being the most important element. The number of stresses in an English line is normally fixed, while the number of syllables may vary; in French verse the reverse is true. In English verse, rhyme can disappear altogether, whereas there is practically no unrhymed French verse before the twentieth century, and even today French poets are reluctant to give up rhyme altogether when writing verse. (The prose poem is of course a separate genre to which none of the remarks in this essay apply). Compare the following example from Shakespeare:

My *thought*, whose *murder yet* is *but* fan*tas*tical,
Shakes *so* my *single state* of *man*, that *func*tion
Is *smoth*ered *in* sur*mise*; and *noth*ing *is*
But what is not.

(Macbeth, 1, 3)

where each full line has five stresses, but the first has twelve syllables, the second eleven, the third ten, and where there is no rhyme, with this couplet from Corneille:

> Ton *nom* ne peut plus *croî*tre, il ne lui *man*que *rien*;
> *Souf*fre qu'un *aut*re *ici* puisse ennob*lir* le *sien*.

(*Horace*, lines 549-50)

where the rhyme is an important element, and although each line contains twelve syllables, the first has four stresses, the second five.

The result of these differences is that English ears find it difficult at first to appreciate the prosodic framework within which French poets operate and to detect the subtleties of the means they use to achieve their ends. It is worth examining each of the three elements in turn.

Rhyme

Rhyme develops from the assonance of medieval poetry (that is, the identity, at the end of lines, of vowel sounds only). The strict rules for rhyme, as for other aspects of versification, were codified at the beginning of the seventeenth century; the name of Malherbe is important in this respect, but the extent of his rôle as initiator is debated.

Alternation

One prescription that was little contested until the end of the nineteenth century, and is still widely observed, is that of alternating rhyme – *l'alternance des rimes*. This is the principle according to which a pair (or set) of masculine rhymes must be followed by a pair (or set) of feminine rhymes. The terms *masculine* and *feminine* in this context often give rise to confusion: it is important to realise that *as applied to rhymes* they have no necessary relation to gender. A feminine rhyme is defined as a word, *regardless of grammatical gender or part of speech,* whose last vowel is a *mute e: alouette* (feminine noun), *squelette* (masculine noun), *fouette* (verb) are all examples of feminine rhyme. A masculine rhyme is any word, again of either gender or none whose final vowel is NOT a *mute e*: for instance, *bruit* (masculine noun), *nuit* (feminine noun or verb), *s'enfuit* (verb). The following example from Hugo's *Odes et Ballades* shows one arrangement of alternating feminine and masculine rhymes in a five line stanza:

J'ai des rêves de guerre en mon âme inquiète!
J'aurais été soldat, si je n'étais poète.
Ne vous étonnez point que j'aime les guerriers!
Souvent, pleurant sur eux, dans ma douleur muette,
J'ai trouvé leur cyprès plus beaux que nos lauriers.

(Mon Enfance)

Degrees of Acceptability of Rhymes

There are a number of rules governing the admissibility or otherwise of certain pairs of rhymes; it is important for the writer to know the detail of these rules, but it is enough for the reader to be aware of the principle that rhymes which are facile or obvious, and therefore likely to be hackneyed, are frowned on, e.g. such pairs as *gloire/victoire, porter/comporter*. Similarly the rhyming of a closed with an open vowel (*trône/couronne, ramasse/grâce*), or of words having the same inflected ending (*pleuvra/reverra, durement/allègrement*) is regarded as a weakness.

On a more positive note, the degree of richness of the rhymes needs to be considered. The French terms here, which are frequently encountered, are *rimes pauvres, rimes suffisantes,* and *rimes riches*; equivalent English terms might be *poor, adequate* and *rich*. Precise definition of these categories varies from one French authority to another; the following are proposed as working definitions only.

For there to exist a rhyme at all, the last vowel of the two rhyming lines must be identical (in this context a final *mute e* does not count as a vowel, so the vowel that precedes it must rhyme), as must any consonants that follow it.

To be *suffisante* or adequate, a rhyme must contain this identical vowel sound plus one other identical phonetic element (normally, though not necessarily, a pronounced consonant). If it does not contain this second rhyming element, it is said to be a *rime pauvre*. If it contains more than one identical element over and above the compulsory rhymed vowel, it is said to be a *rime riche*; it follows that not all rich rhymes are polysyllabic rhymes, since identity of vowel plus two pronounced consonants may constitute a rich rhyme. Following are examples of three types of rhyme, showing the different combinations of vowels and consonants that constitute a minimum fulfilment of the conditions:

rimes pauvres:
    heurt|a / voil|à; cour|us / dess|us
    (no *pronounced* rhyming consonant)

rimes suffisantes:

> cardin|al / lég|al; légère|té / heur|té; vous êtes / squel|ettes
> (vowel plus one *pronounced* rhyming consonant)

rimes riches:

> cardi|nal / ver|nal; gou|dron /esca|dron; s|anté / h|anté
> (in the first two examples: vowel plus *two pronounced*
consonants; in the third, *two vowels* plus one pronounced consonant)

There are a number of terms for rhymes containing rhyming elements greater than the three needed for rich rhyme, the commonest ones being *rime double* and *rime léonine*. Examples:

> card|inal / mat|inal; esp|érance / tol|érance; |l'acier / g|lacier.

Most French poets tend to use such rhymes sparingly, doubtless because they want to avoid being mere virtuosos, but in their *moments perdus* may indulge in such rhyming *tours de force* as the well-known (and variously attributed):

> Gal, amant de la reine, alla, tour magnanime,
> Galamment de l'arène à la Tour Magne, à Nîmes.

Rich rhyme is more often encountered in the work of nineteenth century poets than in previous periods but even here, though it may predominate in a given poem, it is the exception rather than the rule. The best French poets seem to feel that the effect is more impressive for being used with discretion. And occasionally even the most accomplished poet will feel justified in the use of a *rime pauvre* or a rhyme from one of the prohibited categories. An overall effect aimed at may well justify the infringement of a particular rule.

Syllabism

One rule however that no French author of verse poems would feel justified in breaking is the one that regulates the number of syllables in the line; the occurrence of a fixed number of syllables in the line is the basic feature that distinguishes French poetry – both from French prose and from the poetry of practically all other languages.

The counting of Syllables is important, not so much in order to be able to scan verse in the mechanical sense as to be in a position to identify and respond to the rhythms, which will be discussed under the heading of *Accentuation*.

Traditional verse forms in French observe conventions of pronunciation that do not apply to the spoken language of today. The *mute e* always counts in scansion as a pronounced vowel, unless it immediately precedes another vowel or an unaspirated *h*, when it is said to be elided. (This means that the twelve-syllable alexandrine has in fact thirteen syllables when the rhyme is feminine: e.g. *Contemplons à loisir cette caricature*. Few readers of verse today actually pronounce the *mute e*; most slightly lengthen the preceding syllable, but no careful reader of verse ignores it and in traditional musical settings of poems composers normally give it a note value – including the *mute e* of the feminine rhyme ending, which in the speaking of verse is in fact omitted.

In the following examples elided *mute e*'s are shown between parentheses:

> Grand(e) et svelt(e) en marchant comm(e) une chasseresse . .
> Qu'on clou(e) en grande hât(e) un cercueil quelque part . .

There is a convention by which words containing a vowel sound followed immediately by a *mute e* – words like *cloue* in the example above, *plaie, Iphigénie* or *crée* – may be used in the body of a line of verse only when the *mute e* is elided into a following vowel; in the following example, the word *pensée* can be used because it is followed by the initial vowel of *emplit*:

> Une pensée emplit le tumulte superbe.

But its plural, like the forms such as *plaies, crées, cloues* and so on, cannot be used in the body of a line; in the following line, the poet has avoided the difficulty by using the archaic form *pensers*:

> Mille pensers dormaient, chrysalides funèbres . . .

The word *dormaient* in this example illustrates the convention whereby the verb endings *-aient* and the verb form *soient* are regarded as a single syllable for purposes of scansion :

> Le jour qu'on l'entraîna vers l'Afrique abhorrée
> Ses enfants étaient là qui voulaient l'embrasser.

> (Hugo: *Les Martyrs*)

The two semi-vowels [j] and [ɥ], which are found only immediately before vowels (e.g. *lien, patience, nuit, fluide*) are sometimes regarded as vowels, sometimes as consonants. It is important to know which if one is writing verse, but if one is merely scanning then the convention followed by the poet can be determined by scanning the rest of the line. For most words, the convention is fixed (e.g. the *i* in nouns ending in *-sion* and *-tion* counts as a vowel; *imagination* for instance has six syllables); but there are a few words where the poet has a choice. Thus the same poet (François Coppée) can make *hier* into a word of one or two syllables:

> De sa vue, hier encor, je faisais mon délice (one syllable)
> Or, ce fut hier soir, quand elle me parla (two syllables)

Accentuation

Although much less strongly accentuated than English, spoken French does in fact have a perceptible stress accent on the last syllable of each sense-group – or the last but one where the last syllable is a *mute e*. It is this stress accent that gives considerable variety of rhythmic pattern to the alexandrine, though it is a variety that the English ear will only detect by attentive listening over a period of time. As a start we might consider an example purely empirically. In this and later examples, the oblique stroke immediately follows the final syllable of the sense-group, that is to say the final stressed syllable. The numbers at the end of the lines are a schematic representation of the rhythmic pattern. This is a useful practice to observe until the reader is sure he is competent in the instant recognition of rhythmic groups, and it is at all times helpful in revealing significant rhythmic patterns.

> Tu demand/es pourquoi/j'ai tant de rag(e)/ au cœur 3.[e]2.4.2
> Et sur un col/flexibl(e)/une têt(e)/indomptée 4.2.3.3
> C'est que je suis issu/de la rac/e d'Antée, 6.3.[e]2
> Je retourn/e les dards/contre le dieu/vainqueur. 3.[e]2.4.2

(Nerval: *Antéros*)

In the above numerical representation, as in later examples, the symbol [e] represents the unelided *mute e* at the end of a group in which the immediately preceding syllable is accentuated. (In the text of the examples, (e) is an elided *mute e*). This feature has always proved a difficulty in rhythmic analysis: since the French sense-group ends with the stressed vowel the *mute e* that follows it cannot be counted in that group; on the other hand it is certainly not pronounced as part of the following group, but is in fact indicated by a slight pause. The above way of recording it schematically, proposed by Guiraud, comes nearer to representing the realities of spoken verse than the traditional solution of counting such *mute e*'s as though they were fully pronounced members of the following group.

xxii

The Binary or 'Classical' Alexandrine is the line that has a sufficient break in the sense at the sixth syllable for the two main stresses to fall on the sixth and twelfth syllables. Each half-line is called a *hemistich (un hémistiche)*, and the central break is the *caesura (la césure)*. The running-on of sense, or *enjambement*, in such a way as to eliminate the possibility of a pause, whether at the middle or end of the line, is forbidden in classical practice (hence the misleading term 'classical alexandrine'). Where *enjambement* occurs – and even classical poets allow themselves this licence from time to time – the run-on element is known as the *rejet*. The binary form of the alexandrine is by far the most widely used, even by Romantic poets and their successors later in the nineteenth century.

Within the hemistich however there is a wide variety of rhythmic sub-groups, producing varied effects that are intrinsically pleasing and can be exploited by the best poets to heighten the poetic effect. The following six examples give an idea of the variety to be found within the binary division of the line; the caesura is indicated by the double oblique stroke (//), the sub-groups by a single stroke (/):

Un malheur/inconnu// gliss/e parmi les hommes	3.3/1.[e]4
Aucun/ ressentiment// de l'amitié/ passée	2.4/4.2
Roi,/le plus grand/ des rois,//et qui m'est/ le plus cher	1.3.2/3.3
Fuyards,/ blessés,/ mourants// caissons,/ brancards,/ civières	
	2.2.2/2.2.2
Modulant/ tour à tour// sur la lyr/e d'Orphée	3.3/3.[e]2
Les soupirs/de la saint(e)// et les cris/ de la fée	3.3/3.3

Breaks in the sense are not necessarily indicated by punctuation marks; judgement and common sense are required to determine where they occur, and there are frequently occasions where alternative scansions are possible, as in the third of the above examples. The following stanza shows a post-Romantic poet, Baudelaire, using the rhythmic resources of the binary alexandrine with considerable virtuosity to reinforce the effect produced by the imagery:

Quand le ciel bas et lourd pèse comme un couvercle	3.3/1.[e]4
Sur l'esprit gémissant en proie aux longs ennuis	3.3/2.4
Et que de l'horizon embrassant tout le cercle	6/3.3
Il nous verse un jour noir plus triste que les nuits	3.3/2.[e]3

Analysis of the effects produced by the rhythm of these lines may be helped by bearing in mind Grammont's well supported view that all rhythmic sub-groups, however many syllables they contain, *tend* to occupy the same length of time when spoken, so that a long group is spoken faster than a short group. These changes of pace are very important elements in the armoury of expressive devices available to the poet.

Occasional examples occur of what might be called the *misplaced caesura*; in such lines there is one major break, but not at the sixth syllable:

Elle aimait; elle était pauvre, simple et sereine   3/4.[e]4

A further example occurs in line 9 of the sonnet *Recueillement* below. Such lines are certainly binary, though they depart from the division into two *equal* sections that is the classical norm.

The Ternary or 'Romantic' Alexandrine differs from the binary line in having two more or less equally strong breaks; there may be subgroups or not, but in the ternary line, neither of the two breaks occurs in the precise middle of the line. (The correct French term for any break other than that after the sixth syllable is *la coupe*.) The three groups in the ternary line may be of equal length (4.4.4):

Toujours aimer,/ toujours souffrir,/ toujours mourir . . .

(this 'romantic alexandrine' was written by Corneille at the height of the French classical period); and there is Hugo's line from *La Conscience*:

Il vit un œil/ tout grand ouvert/ dans les ténèbres . . .

But a ternary line may just as easily show no regular pattern:

A ces mots,/ on cria haro/ sur le baudet   3.5.4
C'est qu'hier/ tu l'avais touché/ d'un pied agile   3.5.4
D'aut/res, l'horreur de leurs berceaux,/et quelques-uns 1.[e]6.4
Et qui rêv/ent, ainsi qu'un conscrit/ le canon   3.[e]5.3

It is obvious that this freer form of the alexandrine allows an even greater variety of rhythmic patterns and effects; it also produces much more frequent *enjambement* over the line than is associated with the binary alexandrine. Judicious use of the two types of line can produce effects of great subtlety and complexity, especially as the most obvious effect of *enjambement* is to throw great emphasis on the *rejet*, the run-on element.

The following sonnet by Baudelaire exhibits masterly use of all the resources of the alexandrine (the rhythmic patterns just referred to, but also sound-patterns – note particularly the rhymes) employed not to virtuoso effect, but to underpin the poetic effect of vocabulary and images. The poem repays careful analysis of all these effects.

Recueillement

Sois sage, ô ma douleur, et tiens-toi plus tranquille	2.4/3.3
Tu réclamais le Soir; il descend; le voici:	4.2/3.3
Une atmosphère obscure enveloppe la ville,	4.2/3.[e]2
Aux uns portant la paix, aux autres le souci.	2.4/2.[e]3
Pendant que des mortels la multitude vile	6/4.[e]1
Sous le fouet du Plaisir, ce bourreau sans merci	3.3/3.3
Va cueillir des remords dans la fête servile,	3.3/3.[e]2
Ma douleur, donne-moi la main, viens par ici	3/3.2/4
Loin d'eux. Vois se pencher les défuntes Années	2/4.3[e]2
Sur les balcons du ciel, en robes surannées;	4.2/2.[e]3
Surgir du fond des eaux le Regret souriant;	2.4/3.3
Le Soleil moribond s'endormir sous une arche	3.3/3.3
Et, comme un long linceul traînant à l'Orient	1.5/2.4
Entends, ma chère, entends la douce nuit qui marche.	2.2.2/4.2

It will be noted that twelve of the fourteen lines are binary or 'classical'; that even in these there is a great variety of rhythmic effects (especially noticeable is the sort of counterpoint between rhythms tending towards the monotonous – lines 6 and 7 – to reflect the mechanical pursuit of pleasure, and the much subtler rhythms and changes of pace in lines evoking the world of the poet's mind, particularly the last two lines). The poet departs from binary rhythms only in lines 8 and 9 but the effect is very striking: in the first place because the French sonnet normally exhibits a definite break in syntax and sense between the quatrains and the tercets. The sort of *enjambement* therefore that we have here from quatrain to tercet is intrinsically novel, but with *Loin d'eux* strongly emphasised in the run-on position, the poet underlines most effectively the gulf between the pleasure-seeking masses and the figure engaged in solitary contemplation. Close attention to the prosody of this poem will reveal many further significant parallels between the surface meaning, the suggestions lying below the surface, and the sounds and rhythms in which the meanings are realised.

S.W.T.

4. Glossary of Terms used in the Analysis of Poetry

We have aimed to include terms which students may find useful in formulating their own observations, rather than to provide an exhaustive list of terms used by other critics, grammarians and rhetoricians. We should like to emphasise the practical value of technical terms as a kind of shorthand, which enables us to refer precisely to phenomena which it would be unnecessarily time-consuming to describe in full whenever we meet them. There is no virtue in using jargon for its own sake.

The definitions and examples given below relate to the English uses of the words discussed; the parallel French words are not always used in exactly the same way.

ACCUMULATION: The piling up, in a list, of a number of words of the same grammatical kind (noun, verb, adjective), to indicate variety, diversity or multiplicity.

> Oh! dites-moi, ravins, frais ruisseaux, treilles mûres,
> Rameaux chargés de nids, grottes, forêts, buissons,
> Est-ce que vous ferez pour d'autres vos murmures?
>
> (Hugo: *Tristesse d'Olympio*)

> Considérez encor que j'avais dès l'aurore,
> Travaillé, combattu, pensé, marché, lutté.
>
> (Hugo: *A Villequier*)

> Et mon regard long, triste, errant, involontaire,
> Les suivait, et de pleurs sans chagrin s'humectait.
>
> (Lamartine: *L'Occident*)

ALLEGORY: a narrative or description in which characters and actions are consistently used as symbols of, or metaphors for, another, abstract level of meaning (moral, spiritual, political etc.). Personification is often the basis of allegory. (Cf. *Pilgrim's Progress*)

> . . . . sur cette entreprise
> Vint arriver, à toute sa barbe grise,
> Un bon vieillard, portant chère joyeuse,
> Confortatif, de parole amoureuse,
> Bien ressemblant homme de grand renom,

Et s'appelait Bon Espoir par son nom;
Lequel voyant cette femme tremblante,
Autre qu'humaine (à la voir) ressemblante,
Vouloir ainsi mon malheur pourchasser,
Fort rudement s'efforce à la chasser.

(Marot: *L'Epître du Dépourvu*)

ALLITERATION: repetition of the same sound to produce effects of harmony or emphasis; most often refers to initial sounds, but also used of consonants within the word. (Note: according to its derivation from *litera*, alliteration involves repetition of *letters*, but it is the repetition of *sounds* that is most significant in poetry. Repetition of the same letter with different pronunciations, which occurs quite frequently in non-phonetic languages such as English and French, is only of limited importance. Transcription of alliterative lines into International Phonetic Alphabet is a habit worth cultivating to avoid confusion in this respect. (Cf. *Assonance*).

Elle est dans le devoir, tous deux sont dignes d'elle.

(Corneille: *Le Cid*)

Sound patterns sometimes combine alliteration and assonance:

La moisson de nos champs lassera nos faucilles,
Et les fruits passeront la promesse des fleurs.

(Malherbe: *Prière pour le Roi Henri le Grand*)

La princesse, dans un palais de rose pure,
Sous les murmures, sous la mobile ombre dort.

(Valéry: *Au Bois Dormant*)

ANACOLUTHON: interruption of the grammatical construction of a sentence. The parts of the sentence do not fit together grammatically.

Où ces divins esprits, hautains et relevés,
Qui des eaux d'Hélicon ont les sens abreuvés,
De verve et de fureur leur ouvrage étincelle,
De leurs vers tout divins la grâce est naturelle . . .

(Régnier: *Satire IX*)

Mes soldats presque nus, dans l'ombre intimidés,
Les rangs de toutes parts mal pris et mal gardés,
Le désordre partout redoublant les alarmes,

Nous-mêmes contre nous tournant nos propres armes,
Les cris que les rochers renvoyaient plus affreux,
Enfin toute l'horreur d'un combat ténébreux:
Que pouvait la valeur dans ce trouble funeste?

(Racine: *Mithridate*)

ANAPHORA: repetition of the same word or phrase at the beginning of a sequence of grammatically parallel constructions. In poetry this is usually, but not invariably, at the beginning of a series of lines or stanzas.

Puisque j'ai mis ma lèvre à ta coupe encor pleine,
Puisque j'ai dans tes mains posé mon front pâli,
Puisque j'ai respiré parfois la douce haleine
De ton âme, parfum dans l'ombre enseveli,

Puisqu'il me fut donné de t'entendre me dire
Les mots où se répand le cœur mystérieux,
Puisque j'ai vu pleurer, puisque j'ai vu sourire
Ta bouche sur ma bouche et tes yeux sur mes yeux;

Puisque j'ai vu briller sur ma tête ravie
Un rayon de ton astre, hélas! voilé toujours,
Puisque j'ai vu tomber dans l'onde de ma vie
Une feuille de rose arrachée à tes jours,

Je puis maintenant dire aux rapides années:
– Passez! passez toujours! je n'ai plus à vieillir!

(Hugo: *Puisque j'ai mis ma lèvre*)

ANTI-CLIMAX: a lowering of tension or emphasis when a heightening is expected. Unintentional anti-climax is often termed "bathos". (Cf. *Climax*).

Je chante les combats, et ce prélat terrible
Qui par ses longs travaux et sa force invincible,
Dans une illustre église exerçant son grand cœur,
Fit placer à la fin un lutrin dans le chœur.

(Boileau: *Le Lutrin*)

Poem no. 15 in this collection is an example of a complete poem based on anti-climax.

ANTITHESIS: emphasis on the contrast between two words or ideas, usually achieved by placing them in close proximity, often in parallel constructions.

> Le jour est paresseux mais la nuit est active.
>
> > (Eluard: *Notre Mouvement*)
>
> Péri est mort pour ce qui nous fait vivre.
>
> > (Eluard: *Gabriel Péri*)
>
> Suis le jour dans le ciel, suis l'ombre sur la terre.
>
> > (Lamartine: *Le Vallon*)

APOSTROPHE: direct address to a person, or, more frequently, a personified object or concept.

> Grands Bois, vous m'effrayez, comme les cathédrales.
>
> > (Baudelaire: *Obsession*)
>
> O Mort, vieux capitaine, il est temps! levons l'ancre.
>
> > (Baudelaire: *Le Voyage*)
>
> O temps, suspends ton vol! et vous, heures propices,
> Suspendez votre cours.
>
> > (Lamartine: *Le Lac*)

ASSONANCE: a repetition of the same sound in different words, for effects of harmony or emphasis; normally used of vowel sounds, and especially of the final stressed vowels in lines of poetry. (The medieval *Chanson de Roland*, for example, is written in *assonating* verse: the lines of each *laisse* or stanza have the same final stressed vowel but different consonants; they *assonate*, but do not rhyme). (Cf. *Alliteration*).

> Quand du stérile hiver a resplendi l'ennui.
>
> > (Mallarmé: *Le vierge, le vivace et le bel aujourd'hui*)

Sound patterns are sometimes a mixture of assonance and alliteration:

> La princesse, dans un palais de rose pure,
> Sous les murmures, sous la mobile ombre dort.
>
> > (Valéry: *Au Bois Dormant*)

CHIASMUS: a symmetry of expression in which the order of the first part is reversed in the second. If the second part is written below the first, the words or ideas linked form the X-shape of the Greek letter *chi*.

Ils ne mouraient pas tous, mais tous étaient frappés.

(La Fontaine: *Les Animaux Malades de la Peste*)

Pleurez, doux halcyons, ô vous, oiseaux sacrés,
Oiseaux chers à Thétis, doux alcyons, pleurez.

(Chénier: *La Jeune Tarentine*)

CIRCUMLOCUTION: a *roundabout* way of speaking: indirect reference to an object or action by a phrase instead of a single word. *Circumlocution* usually has pejorative connotations, suggesting an unnecessary and unproductive long-windedness. (Cf. *Periphrasis*).

Que Dieu guide à son but la vapeur foudroyante
Sur le fer des chemins qui traversent les monts,
Qu'un Ange soit debout sur sa forge bruyante,
Quand elle va sous terre ou fait trembler les ponts,
Et, de ses dents de fer dévorant les chaudières,
Transperce les cités et saute les rivières,
Plus vite que le cerf dans l'ardeur de ses bonds!

Oui, si l'Ange aux yeux bleus ne veille sur sa route,
Et le glaive à la main ne plane et la défend,
S'il n'a compté les coups du levier, s'il n'écoute
Chaque tour de la roue en son cours triomphant,
S'il n'a l'œil sur les eaux et la main sur la braise,
Pour jeter en éclats la magique fournaise,
Il souffrira toujours du caillou d'un enfant.

(Vigny: *La Maison du Berger*)

CLIMAX: a building-up of effects to a high point. (Cf. *Anti-climax*)

On fit donc une fosse, et Caïn dit: "C'est bien!"
Puis il descendit seul sous cette voûte sombre:
Quand il se fut assis sur sa chaise dans l'ombre
Et qu'on eut sur son front fermé le souterrain,
L'œil était dans la tombe et regardait Caïn.

(Hugo: *La Conscience*)

CONCEIT: an ingenious expression of an idea, normally based on an image and frequently making use of paradox or hyperbole; a conceit appeals to the intellect rather than to the imagination.

> D'un air plein d'amoureuse flamme,
> Aux accents de ta douce voix,
> Je vois les fleuves et les bois
> S'embraser comme a fait mon âme.

(Théophile de Viau: La Solitude)

HYPERBOLE: exaggeration, for the purpose of emphasis; the reader is not expected to take a hyperbolic statement as the literal truth. (Cf. Understatement).

> Mon âme est dans les fers, mon sang est dans la flamme,
> Jamais malheur ne fut à mon malheur égal.

Théophile de Viau: Désespoirs Amoureux)

> O toute parfaite princesse,
> L'étonnement de l'univers,
> Astre par qui vont avoir cesse
> Nos ténèbres et nos hivers,
> Exemple sans autres exemples,
> Future image de nos temples!

(Malherbe: Ode à la Reine pour sa bienvenue en France)

Sometimes the gap between literal truth and hyperbolic expression is deliberately exploited as a source of irony.

> Devant moi justement on plante un grand potage,
> D'où les mouches à jeun se sauvaient à la nage.

(Régnier: Satire XI)

> Je ne suis plus vivant, je ne sers que de nombre,
> Sinon que mes soupirs découvrent que je vis.

Théophile de Viau: Désespoirs Amoureux)

IMAGE: an object, not present, made to seem perceptible by any of the senses.

> Bergère, ô Tour Eiffel, le troupeau des ponts bêle ce matin.

(Apollinaire: Zone)

Contemple-les, mon âme, ils sont vraiment affreux!
Pareils aux mannequins; vaguement ridicules;
Terribles, singuliers comme les somnambules;
Dardant on ne sait où leurs globes ténébreux.

(Baudelaire: *Les Aveugles*)

Le soleil prolongeait sur la cime des tentes
Ces obliques rayons, ces flammes éclatantes,
Ces larges traces d'or qu'il laisse dans les airs,
Lorsqu'en un lit de sable il se couche aux déserts.

(Vigny: *Moïse*)

In a narrower sense, *image* and *imagery* are terms used for non-literal forms of expression: metaphor, metonymy, simile, symbol etc.

INVERSION: reversal of normal word order for effects of rhyme, rhythm or emphasis. In poetry this refers not so much to the inversion of the subject and verb, which is to a large extent governed by the grammatical rules, as to prepositional phrases which are displaced so as to precede, rather than follow, the word they qualify.

O reine,ô de Minos épouse désolée.

(Chénier: *Pasiphaé*)

L'art, des transports de l'âme est un faible interprète.

(Chénier: *L'Art. . .*)

J'aime de vos longs yeux la lumière verdâtre.

(Baudelaire: *Chant d'Automne*)

IRONY: communication to the reader of a meaning different from the ostensible meaning of the words used, and often its direct opposite. It is often clearest when speaker and hearer are created characters in the poem.

Monsieur Napoléon, c'est son nom authentique,
Est pauvre et même prince; il aime les palais;
Il lui convient d'avoir des chevaux, des valets,
De l'argent pour son jeu, sa table, son alcôve,
Ses chasses; par la même occasion il sauve
La famille, l'église et la société.

(Hugo: *Souvenir de la Nuit du Quatre*)

METAPHOR: the explicit expression of resemblance, without the use of words which suggest comparison. The literal meaning is sometimes expressed, sometimes not.

> Ne pourrons-nous jamais, sur l'océan des âges
> Jeter l'ancre un seul jour?
>
> (Lamartine: *Le Lac*)

> Ma jeunesse ne fut qu'un ténébreux orage.
>
> (Baudelaire: *L'Ennemi*)

> Ces fleurs dont le printemps fait voir tes rives peintes.
>
> (Théophile de Viau: *Proche de la saison*)

METONYMY: the representation of a person, object or concept by one of its attributes. (Like metaphor, metonymy involves a *substitution* of one term for another).

> La moisson de nos champs lassera nos faucilles.
>
> (Malherbe: *Prière pour le Roi Henri le Grand*)

ONOMATOPOEIA: the use of a word or words whose sound appears to imitate the sound of the thing they represent. The use of sound patterns to evoke an emotional response similar to that produced by the subject-matter is not true onomatopoeia.

> Pour qui sont ces serpents qui sifflent sur vos têtes?
>
> (Racine: *Andromaque*)

> A grand bruit et à grand fracas
> Un torrent tombait des montagnes:
> Tout fuyait devant lui; l'horreur suivait ses pas.
>
> (La Fontaine: *Le Torrent et la Rivière*)

> Les mânes effrayés quittent leurs monuments;
> L'air retentit au loin de leurs longs hurlements,
> Et les vents, échappés de leurs cavernes sombres,
> Mêlent à leurs clameurs d'horribles sifflements.
>
> (Jean-Baptiste Rousseau: *Circé*)

OXYMORON: the bringing together in a close grammatical relationship, like that of a noun with adjective or verb with adverb, of words with opposite meaning.

> Cette sombre clarté qui tombe des étoiles.

> (Corneille: *Le Cid*)

> Victorieusement fui le suicide beau.

> (Mallarmé: '*Victorieusement fui . . .*')

PARADOX: originally, an idea or a statement contrary to received opinion. Nowadays, more generally used of a statement which is apparently self-contradictory, but expresses an underlying truth.

> J'écoute à demi transporté
> Le bruit des ailes du silence
> Qui volent dans l'obscurité.

> (Saint-Amant: *Le Contemplateur*)

> Il tua tous ceux qui le suivaient, après la chasse ou les libations.
> – Tous le suivaient.
> Il s'amusa à égorger les bêtes de luxe.
> Il fit flamber le palais.
> Il se ruait sur les gens et les taillait en pièces.
> – La foule, les toits d'or, les belles bêtes existaient encore.

> (Rimbaud: *Conte*)

PARATAXIS: the placing of clauses or sentences one after the other without words to indicate syntactical coordination or subordination.

> Je vis cette faucheuse. Elle était dans son champ.
> Elle allait à grands pas moissonnant et fauchant.

> (Hugo: *Mors*)

Prévert's *Inventaire* (Poem no. 73) is a good example of a complete poem built up in this way.

PATHETIC FALLACY: the belief, typically expressed through personification, that Nature genuinely participates in and reflects the emotions, joys and sorrows of mankind.

Que le vent qui gémit, le roseau qui soupire,
Que les parfums légers de ton air embaumé,
Que tout ce qu'on entend, l'on voit ou l'on respire,
Tout dise: "Ils ont aimé!"

(Lamartine: *Le Lac*)

PERIPHRASIS: essentially the same as circumlocution, but the term *periphrasis* is more often used when the positive values of 'roundabout' expressions are to be emphasised. Periphrasis is often used to give elevation or nobility to an idea (a device much abused in the eighteenth century), but it may also concentrate attention on particular attributes of a concept.

Le sommeil du tombeau pressera ma paupière.

(Chénier: *Iambes*)

Et le char vaporeux de la reine des ombres.

(Lamartine: *L'Isolement*)

PERSONIFICATION: the attribution of human actions, emotions or characteristics to animals, inanimate objects or abstract qualities. Extended personification is often the basis of allegory.

La mort a des rigueurs à nulle autre pareilles;
On a beau la prier;
La cruelle qu'elle est se bouche les oreilles,
Et nous laisse crier.

(Malherbe: *Consolation à M. du Périer*)

REPETITION: for purposes of harmony or emphasis a word, phrase or grammatical construction may be repeated. (Cf. Assonance and Alliteration).

Rappelez-lui souvent, rappelez-lui toujours
Néère tout son bien, Néère ses amours;
Cette Néère, hélas, qu'il nommait sa Néère.

(Chénier: *Néère*)

Les champs n'étaient point noirs, les cieux n'étaient pas mornes

(Hugo: *Tristesse d'Olympio*)

Sur mes cahiers d'écolier
Sur mon pupitre et les arbres
Sur le sable sur la neige
J'écris ton nom.

Sur toutes les pages lues
Sur toutes les pages blanches
Pierre sang papier ou cendre
J'écris ton nom.

(Eluard: Liberté)

RHETORICAL QUESTION: a question asked for effect, when an answer is either not expected or impossible.

> Ne sentirai-je plus de charme qui m'arrête?
> Ai-je passé le temps d'aimer?

(La Fontaine: Les Deux Pigeons)

> Plonger au fond du gouffre, Enfer ou Ciel, qu'importe?

(Baudelaire: Le Voyage)

SIMILE: an imaginative comparison, usually relating something specific to something more general. Like metaphor, simile is founded on resemblance, but it is more explicit. (Note: the French *comparaison* is used in this sense, e.g. *he swims like a fish*, and also to denote a purely factual comparison, e.g. *he swims like his brother*).

> Comme un dernier rayon, comme un dernier zéphyre
> Anime la fin d'un beau jour,
> Au pied de l'échafaud j'essaye encor ma lyre.

(Chénier: Iambes)

> Quand le ciel bas et lourd pèse comme un couvercle.

(Baudelaire: Spleen)

SYMBOL: an object that may be recognised as standing for something else. The relationship may be one that is universally recognised (for example, the clock in Baudelaire's *L'Horloge* symbolises the passage of time), or it may be an original creation, either explicit, as in Gautier's *Le Pot de Fleurs* (poem no.36) or implicit, as in the poetry of the Symbolists, where its interpretation demands of the reader an imagination parallel to that of the poet.

SYNAESTHESIA: the process by which impressions received through different senses are linked and intermingled. The best-known examples of these are provided by Baudelaire in his influential poem *Correspondances*:

> . . .
> Comme de longs échos qui de loin se confondent
> Dans une ténébreuse et profonde unité,
> Vaste comme la nuit et comme la clarté,
> Les parfums, les couleurs et les sons se répondent.
>
> Il est des parfums frais comme des chairs d'enfants,
> Doux comme les hautbois, verts comme les prairies,
> – Et d'autres, corrompus, riches et triomphants,
>
> Ayant l'expansion des choses infinies,
> Comme l'ambre, le musc, le benjoin et l'encens,
> Qui chantent les transports de l'esprit et des sens.

Cf. also Verlaine:

> Je devine, à travers un murmure,
> Le contour subtil des voix anciennes
> Et dans les lueurs musiciennes,
> Amour pâle, une aurore future!
>
> (*Ariettes oubliées*)

In some cases the different sense-impressions are less closely fused; the following example may be construed as three separate sense-impressions in a single grammatical construction, although this does not necessarily preclude an element of synaesthetic interaction between them:

> Un froid et ténébreux silence
> Dort à l'ombre de ces ormeaux.
>
> (Théophile de Viau: *La Solitude*)

UNDERSTATEMENT: the device of saying less than one means, inviting the reader to 'read between the lines'. Like its opposite, hyperbole, understatement is often associated with irony and wit.

> L'insensible et le froid Voiture
> Parlait d'amour comme s'il en sentait.
>
> Mais un faune qui l'entendit
> Aux Dryades se prit à dire:
> "Possible est-il plus vrai qu'il ne le dit."
>
> (Voiture: *La terre brillante de fleurs*)

Je te plais tu me plais et c'était dans la manche
Et les grands sentiments n'étaient pas de rigueur.

(Brassens: *Les Amours d'Antan*)

Michaux's *Les Emanglons* (Poem no. 70) is perhaps an example of a whole poem based on understatement.

WIT: self-conscious cleverness, which flatters the reader who is able to appreciate it; it may also involve an awareness of the discrepancy between thought and expression (Cf. *Irony*). Wit is a more sophisticated and more purely intellectual quality than humour.

C'était dans la nuit brune,
Sur le clocher jauni,
    La lune,
Comme un point sur un i.

(Musset: *Ballade à la Lune*)

Non, je ne trouve point beaucoup de différence
De prendre du tabac à vivre d'espérance,
Car l'un n'est que fumée, et l'autre n'est que vent.

(Saint-Amant: *Assis sur un fagot . . .*)

ZEUGMA: the linking together in a single grammatical construction of words that stand in different relationships to the word that introduces the construction. (Frequently the word or phrase that introduces the construction is being used literally in relation to one of its dependents, and metaphorically in relation to the other).

Vêtu de probité candide et de lin blanc.

(Hugo: *Booz Endormi*)

Sous le faix du fagot aussi bien que des ans.

(La Fontaine: *La Mort et le Bûcheron*)

M.J.O'R.
S.A.W.

5. Specimen Commentaries.

I

François Villon, 1431-1463?

L'Epitaphe Villon

Frères humains qui après nous vivez,
N'ayez les cœurs contre nous endurcis,
Car, si pitié de nous pauvres avez,
Dieu en aura plus tôt de vous merci.
5 Vous nous voyez ci attachés cinq, six:
Quant de la chair, que trop avons nourrie,
Elle est piéça dévorée et pourrie,
Et nous, les os, devenons cendre et poudre.
De notre mal personne ne s'en rie;
10 Mais priez Dieu que tous nous veuille absoudre !

Si frères vous clamons, pas n'en devez
Avoir dédain, quoi que fûmes occis
Par justice. Toutefois vous savez
Que tous hommes n'ont pas bon sens rassis;
15 Excusez-nous, puisque sommes transis,
Envers le fils de la Vierge Marie,
Que sa grâce ne soit pour nous tarie,
Nous préservant de l'infernale foudre.
Nous sommes morts, âme ne nous harie;
20 Mais priez Dieu que tous nous veuille absoudre !

La pluie nous a débués et lavés,
Et le soleil desséchés et noircis;
Pies, corbeaux nous ont les yeux cavés,
Et arraché la barbe et les sourcils.
25 Jamais, nul temps nous ne sommes assis;
Puis çà, puis là, comme le vent varie,
A son plaisir sans cesser nous charrie,
Plus becquetés d'oiseaux que dés à coudre.
Ne soyez donc de notre confrérie;
30 Mais priez Dieu que tous nous veuille absoudre !

Prince Jésus, qui sur tous as maîtrie,
Garde qu'Enfer n'ait de nous seigneurie:
A lui n'ayons que faire ni que souldre.
Hommes, ici n'a point de moquerie;
35 Mais priez Dieu que tous nous veuille absoudre !

(Poésies diverses)

xxxix

5	ci : ici
7	piéça : depuis longtemps
8	poudre : poussière
11	clamons : appelons
12	occis : tués
15	transis : raides, morts
19	harie : tourmente
21	débués : lessivés
23	cavés : creusés
31	maîtrie : maîtrise
33	souldre : payer

Possible comparisons : 22, 24, 35, 42, 79

The poem known as the *Epitaphe Villon* or *Ballade des Pendus* does not form part of either of Villon's major works, the *Lais* or the *Testament*, but is one of the sixteen poems designated as *Poésies diverses* by Longnon and subsequent modern editors. Clément Marot, in his edition of Villon's works published in 1533, gave this poem the following title: *L'epitaphe en forme de ballade que feit Villon pour luy et pour ses compagnons, s'attendant estre pendu avec eulx*. It may be this that prompted Longnon to date the poem to 1462-63, since it was late in 1462 that Villon, having been involved in a street brawl, was condemned *à estre pendu et estranglé*, a sentence commuted on appeal (5 January 1463 new style) to ten years' banishment from Paris. While there is nothing implausible about such a dating, it presupposes a more direct connection between life and poetry than may be justified. Even allowing such a connection, our knowledge of Villon's life being far from complete, there could be no certainty that this was the only occasion when the poet was condemned to death.

In any case, despite Marot's explanatory title, the poem is not about the imminent prospect of the gallows. Elsewhere we find in Villon's poetry much tormented contemplation of the agony of the process of dying, the pains of death in the literal and physical sense, but in this poem his imagination has made a leap forward, beyond this stage, so that the voice speaking to us here is that of a man already dead. The poem consists of the words uttered by a corpse hanging from a gibbet, making an appeal to the living – to us – for sympathy and for prayer of intercession that God may forgive him and his fellow-victims. The shape and structure of this appeal are determined by the poetic form of the *ballade*.

The literary convention of the fifteenth century made the ballad a very rigid framework, comprising three stanzas followed by an *envoi* (i.e. a dedication to a patron, real or fictional). Each stanza, and the *envoi*, ends with the same line, called a refrain. The stanza is designated by contemporary theorists as isometric. This term does not merely mean, as in later usage, that all lines are of the same length, but relates to stanza form: the number of syllables in the line must equal the number of lines in the stanza. In the case of this poem, the lines are decasyllabic and the stanzas are therefore ten lines long (the *envoi* is usually shorter, as here). Not merely the same rhyme-scheme but the same rhymes must be used in all stanzas, and in the *envoi*, so that in this case the whole poem is built on four rhymes, symmetrically arranged: *ababbccdcd (envoi : ccdcd)*. The convention of alternating masculine and feminine rhymes has not yet been established, but Villon typically, as here, strikes a balance: *a* and *b* are masculine, *c* and *d* feminine. To conform to these various constraints obviously demands at the least a high level of technical proficiency in versification, and a proper assessment of Villon's achievement must take into account his mastery of the form, his poetic craftsmanship. Nowhere in the ballad is there any appearance of contrivance or effort.*

Concealed art characterises the poem at all levels: the dead man's appeal is urgent, natural, even colloquial, yet structured in accordance with the formal framework of the ballad. The first stanza embodies three ideas: appeal to the living (1-4); plight of the dead bodies (5-8); urgent request for prayers (9-10). Each of these is developed in order; stanza 2 – the appeal; stanza 3 – the plight; *envoi* – prayers. In a sense the first stanza is a microcosm of the whole poem, its proportions being taken up as well as its theme. To lines 1-4 and 5-8 correspond a whole stanza, to lines 9-10 corresponds the *envoi*, half the length.

The poem is an appeal. It opens with a direct address, *Frères humains*; and the resonances and implications of these two words will emerge as the poem unfolds. They provide two thematic keys. *Frères* relates to the idea of brotherhood, here conceived in the Christian sense, that we are all children of a common Father, and this aspect dominates the whole poem, which is specifically a request, meaningless except in a Christian and Catholic context, to the living to intercede for the dead that they may be absolved from their sins.

*This mastery almost certainly extends to the effects of sonority (note for example the repeated [u] sounds of the refrain) but the great differences between Middle French and Modern French pronunciation preclude discussion of the aesthetic effects of sound-patterns in this case.

That is what the refrain, the repeated line, says. This formulation in the third person gives a false emphasis however, for the dominant pronouns throughout are *vous* and *nous*. The word *frères* is taken up and repeated at the start of the second stanza, and echoed in *confrérie* (29). In the same way the word *humains* echoes through the poem, taken up in the second stanza, *tous hommes* (14), and above all, at the climactic conclusion of the poem, in strong and emphatic position at the beginning of line 34. We are being appealed to not just as fellow-believers, but as human beings, even more as humane beings, and the appeal is directed at the whole of mankind.

In this first stanza the expression is rich in religious associations, in scriptural and liturgical parallels. The words of the hanging man to those who pass by have many affinities with the words which the liturgy of Good Friday puts into the mouth of the crucified Christ: *O vos omnes qui transitis per viam, attendite et videte si est dolor similis sicut dolor meus* – 'O all ye that pass by, behold and see if there be any sorrow like unto my sorrow'. In both cases there is a direct address: *vos = vous*, and use of imperatives, and in both cases the visual impact of the sight of suffering is stressed: *videte* cf. *vous nous voyez* (5). There are two scriptural echoes in the first few lines: *harden not your hearts* (2) and lines 3-4 which recall the Beatitudes, *Blessed are the merciful, for they shall obtain mercy*. More generally, the emotional charge of the appeal is very strong. All the associations of *frères, humains, cœurs, pitié, nous pauvres, merci* work together to arouse the sympathy of, not *those who live on* but *you who live after us*.

So far, in a linear reading of the poem (and bearing in mind that, so far as is known, it was left untitled by Villon himself), the identity of the speaker has not been revealed. But at line 5 the picture (literally, *vous nous voyez*) becomes plain. What occurs here is not a transition, nor even an antithesis between the spiritual and the physical but a progression. The living are the more likely to be moved by the present spectacle of the dead bodies, and the sight of what is happening to them. This is certainly how the poet himself typically reacts. A child of his age, he has an obsessive horrified fascination at the physical aspects of death and dying. Death was in his day a common spectacle, executions were public, and the Parisian gibbet of Montfaucon was never empty, so there is here a clear allusion to observed and experienced reality. The experience of the modern reader does not normally embrace the sight of skeletons rotting on the gallows. But Villon recreates the scene with immediacy: *vous nous voyez ci*, a scene of horror if we actually attend to his words.

The strong spiritual and religious character of the first four lines might tempt us to take *chair* (6) in its religious sense (as in *The spirit is willing but the flesh is weak*) and the qualifying phrase *que trop avons nourrie* could point in the same direction, implying over-indulgence in pleasure and sensual gratification; but line 7 removes that ambiguity and presents us with the dreadful physical reality, the long process whereby the bodies on the gibbet remain until nothing is left of them. Perhaps that is why it is impossible to be quite sure how many are hanging there. Is it five or six? The whole stanza moves towards a climax of emotional intensity. The tone of appeal gives way in line 9 to one of warning: *Let no one mock . . .*, and with the refrain the distinction between the living and the dead, so far clearly marked by the contrast between *nous* and *vous* and related verb-forms, first and second person plural, disappears: pray that God may absolve us all, you the living as well as us the dead. The opening words, *frères humains*, now begin to take on their full meaning. As human beings we shall not mock; as brothers, fellow-Christians, we too need absolution, for as fellow-men we too must surely die.

The voice that is speaking to us uses language of the utmost directness and simplicity. There are no figures of rhetoric, no departures from normal and natural word-order or syntax or vocabulary. Even the biblical and liturgical elements are part of the common stock of popular pious expressions. This characteristic of simple plainness is particularly noticeable at the start of the second stanza, where the sense overflows the line endings (11-12-13 and 13-14) producing the effect of a spontaneously natural utterance. At the same time, though we may not notice it, a rhetorical plan is being followed. The speaker forestalls a possible objection on the part of his hearers, and in doing so strengthens his argument and reinforces his appeal. In a sense he is pleading the case for himself and his fellow-victims and so he uses devices of forensic oratory, but concealed under the outward appearances of informality and spontaneous effusion. From the seeming flood of words with which the stanza begins we may single out three: *frères, dédain, justice*. Hardly less insistent than the emphasis on brotherhood and humanity are the warnings against mockery or contempt for the dead. *Dédain* takes up the thought of line 9, and makes it more personal; the generalised, third-person warning is now directed straight at us. It is by avoiding scorn and contempt that we shall show ourselves to be truly brothers. From the forensic point of view the speaker's admission that he and his fellows have met their just fate is important because it is instantly turned back on us. There is a strong pause following the *enjambement* of 11-12 . . . *occis/Par justice*. The next sentence, conversational in tone, calls us to witness (*vous savez*) not, as we might expect, the sinfulness and guilt of those justly condemned, but the lack of good sense (a euphemistic way of saying sinfulness) of all men, *tous hommes*, us as well as the criminals on the gibbet. *Tous hommes* takes us back to the refrain, *tous nous*. The difference is in degree, not in kind. We too need to think about our just deserts, about the four Last Things (Death, Judgement, Hell and Heaven) as they may affect us, as well as others. This thought, developing line 4, should move us to pray for those who, being dead (*transis*, 15) are no longer able to pray for themselves. The designation of Christ as the Son of the Virgin carries forward this same idea, for the Virgin, infinitely compassionate, never fails to intercede for sinners who call upon her assistance. Christ, as God, may be a just judge, but the Virgin's prayers will ensure that her Son tempers justice with mercy, of which we all stand in need (cf. 3-4) if we are to escape Hell.

Given the subject of the poem, it is remarkable that the word *morts* occurs only once (19). The language, as we have seen, has hardly been indirect or evasive, but the plain, blunt statement, *nous sommes morts*, ensures that this stanza too ends on a climax of emotional intensity. This is the stanza of the soul, so it is fitting that that word too should appear in the final injunction before the refrain, *âme ne nous harie*. The refrain now acquires a new tonality. In stanza 1 mocking laughter was to give precedence to prayer for forgiveness of sins. By the end of the second stanza the implication is rather that the dead should be allowed to rest in peace, spared further torment. The prayer is to be for the repose of the soul.

But if stanza 2 was the soul's, stanza 3 is the body's. Developing line 6-8 it confronts us, the living, with a picture of the dead. It forces our eyes to look at the spectacle, but the dead are not set before us merely as hanging skeletons. They are helpless victims, totally at the mercy of the elements – rain, sun and wind – and of the birds of the air wheeling around the gallows. This, characteristically for Villon, is not a picture in the static sense, but a scene of action. The bones themselves may be powerless and helpless, but they are assailed on every side. An accumulation of participles verbally recreates the subjection of the corpses to outside forces acting on them: *débués, lavés, desséchés, noircis, cavés, arraché, becquetés*. All these things have happened to them. As the stanza ends there comes the one simile in the poem; a homely comparison, not an ennobling or beautifying one (28). The message to the living is plain, and is spelled out in line 29. *Confrérie* is the key word here; it echoes *frères*, it refers specifically in context to the band of hanged men, but it is also the word for a criminal gang, such as the *Coquille* of which Villon himself appears to have been a member . . . .

The *envoi*, addressed to *Prince Jésus*, has the character of a prayer. The hanged men, albeit criminals, albeit justly put to death (12-13), like the Good Thief, recognise Christ and reject the lordship of

Hell. Whatever their shortcomings, whatever their crimes they are not Hell's vassals – the word *seigneurie* has clear feudal overtones – but acknowledge Christ as the Lord and Master of all men, *qui sur tous a maîtrie*; note yet again the word *tous*. As the poem ends, for a fourth and final time the voice proclaims the seriousness of the matter. But whereas in the comparable position in the three preceding stanzas it was we who were called on not to mock, now the voice asserts that he is speaking in (literally) deadly earnest. Again there is a fruitful ambiguity in line 34: *here*, in this poem, and *here*, on the gallows, there is no room for jesting. If we are really men – *hommes* – we shall know this.

By the end of the poem it is difficult to resist a biographical interpretation. Villon, who elsewhere (at the end of the *Testament*) calls himself *le bon follâtre*, who there takes his leave swearing *sur son couillon*, who elsewhere finds it possible to laugh at the gallows itself:

> Je suis François, dont il me poise
> Né de Paris, emprés Pontoise,
> Et de la corde d'une toise,
> Saura mon col que mon cul poise . . . .

. . . Villon, in this poem at least, wants the hearer to be in no doubt that he means what he is saying, that he wants his appeal to be heard. Yet if we reflect, this poem is just as much an imaginative projection as the *Ballade pour prier Notre Dame*, where he puts himself inside the mind and the heart of his aged, illiterate mother, or the *Regrets de la Belle Heaulmière*, where he sympathetically recreates the sensibility of the old prostitute lamenting her former life and lost beauty. The voice in this poem is not that of a man facing hanging; nor yet of a soul speaking from the tomb. Villon does not need imagery, because he has imagination; and the daring, arresting imagination of this poem is to give a heap of rotting bones the power of speech. In a sense the whole poem could be regarded as a metaphor of the reaction that the living ought to have when looking at corpses on a gibbet. But such an interpretation would hardly do justice to the immediacy of the spectacle that it creates and the urgency of the appeal that is uttered. Can these bones live? In this poem they do, yet if they live and speak, their message reaches and touches us because we are never in any doubt that they are dead. Villon's age was utterly different from ours; Villon, scholar, poet and jailbird, is not a character whose life and circumstances have much in common with ours. But he has universality because, from his strange, alien experience, he distils the anguish of the human condition, the common lot of all mankind.

T.D.H.

II

André Chénier, 1762-1794

Salut, ô belle nuit

Salut, ô belle nuit, étincelante et sombre,
. . . .
Qui n'entends que la voix de mes vers, et les cris
De la rive aréneuse où se brise Thétis.
Muse, Muse nocturne, apporte-moi ma lyre.
Comme un fier météore, en ton brûlant délire,
Lance-toi dans l'espace; et pour franchir les airs
Prends les ailes des vents, les ailes des éclairs,
Les bonds de la comète aux longs cheveux de flamme.
Mes vers impatients élancés de mon âme
Veulent parler aux dieux, et volent où reluit
L'enthousiasme errant, fils de la belle nuit.
Accours, grande nature, ô mère du génie.
Accours, reine du monde, éternelle Uranie,
Soit que tes pas divins sur l'astre du Lion
Ou sur les triples feux du superbe Orion
Marchent, ou soit qu'au loin, fugitive emportée,
Tu suives les détours de la voie argentée,
Soleils amoncelés dans le céleste azur
Où le peuple a cru voir les traces d'un lait pur;
Descends, non, porte-moi sur ta route brûlante;
Que je m'élève au ciel comme une flamme ardente.
Déjà ce corps pesant se détache de moi.
Adieu, tombeau de chair, je ne suis plus à toi.
Terre, fuis sous mes pas. L'éther où le ciel nage
M'aspire. Je parcours l'océan sans rivage.
Plus de nuit. Je n'ai plus d'un globe opaque et dur
Entre le jour et moi l'impénétrable mur.
Plus de nuit, et mon œil et se perd et se mêle
Dans les torrents profonds de lumière éternelle.
Me voici sur les feux que le langage humain
Nomme Cassiopée et l'Ourse et le Dauphin.
Maintenant la Couronne autour de moi s'embrase.
Ici l'Aigle et le Cygne et la Lyre et Pégase.
Et voici que plus loin le Serpent tortueux
Noue autour de mes pas ses anneaux lumineux.
Féconde immensité, les esprits magnanimes
Aiment à se plonger dans les vivants abîmes;
Abîmes de clarté, où, libre de ses fers,

40   L'homme siège au conseil qui créa l'univers;
          Où l'âme remontant à sa grande origine
          Sent qu'elle est une part de l'essence divine.

(L'Amérique)

Possible comparison : 55

André Chénier's situation in literary history is complex. His poetry in some respects follows the French Classical tradition, renewed in the eighteenth century by archeological rediscovery of Antiquity. It belongs also to a rational age interested in the diffusion of scientific knowledge. At the same time, its individual expression of personal emotions makes Chénier a forerunner of the Romantic poets.

This is one of the fragments of Chénier's unfinished poem *L'Amérique*. It was to be a long narrative and didactic work, a story of the conquest of Spanish America, combined with a history and geography of the world. At Chénier's death by guillotine in 1794, this, together with many other poems, was uncompleted and unpublished.

This passage is a sequence of alexandrine couplets (the second line unwritten), which was to be sung at the end of an open air banquet at night, by one of the poem's principal characters, the poet Alonzo d'Ercilla. The first part (lines 1-22) is a series of invocations, and in the second part (lines 23-42) the poet imagines himself, in his inspired state, to be borne aloft among the stars.

The first sentence is an apostrophe to night, dark and silent. But the atmosphere is not grim or gloomy. The first words set the tone: *salut* is a joyful greeting and the night is beautiful. The darkness is not total but *étincelante* (with the brilliance of stars) and the silence is broken by the sounds of the poet's song and of the breaking of waves on the beach, sounds which are given life by the words *voix* and *cris*. In lines 3 and 4 the harmony of Chénier's words is especially effective. There are alliterations of [v] and [r]. In particular the group [ri] in *cris, rive* and *brise,* and the [ar] in *la rive* and *aréneuse,* form patterns of repetition which suggest the regular rhythm of the waves. The learned, latinate word *aréneuse* (sandy) and the name of Thétis (chief of the Nereids, or sea-nymphs) used, as it was by Latin poets, simply to mean "the sea", have a certain classical nobility.

Classical antiquity is again evoked in line 5 with the apostrophe to the Muse and the reference to the lyre, the attribute or symbol of the poet. The word *Muse* is at first unqualified, but the repetition is made more specific by the addition of the adjective *nocturne*. This is a night Muse who is called on to inspire the poet, but we are not yet told which of the Muses she is. This call is more insistant than the greeting to night and the assonance of [y] sounds perhaps reinforces this.

After this short sentence comes a longer one in which the excitement increases as the poetic frenzy of the muse is visualised. Lines 6 to 9 are full of light and movement. The light (*météore, brûlant, éclairs, comète, flamme*) has expanded from its source, the word *étincelante* in the first line, a glimmer in the darkness of night. The movement (*météore, lance-toi, franchir les airs, ailes, vents, éclairs, bonds*) has expanded from the rhythmical movement of the waves. It is no longer a movement on the level of sea and land but a flight through space. Its impetus is helped by repetition of *les ailes des* and the assonance of close and open e's in lines 7 and 8. The phenomena of the sky here are winds and lightning, and the meteor, more distant though somewhat humanised by the adjective *fier*, and the comet whose long flaming hair also gives a partly humanised beauty.

In lines 10 to 12 the excited movement is that of the poet's verses; the frenzy is the poet's, not the Muse's. Poetry is the product of the soul and has a natural affinity with the divine, and so rushes skywards. The *enjambement* of subject and verb in lines 10 and 11 and of verb and subject inverted in lines 11 and 12 accentuates the onward flow. Again there is brightness, that of Enthusiasm (*où reluit / L'Enthousiasme*), the celestial source of the poet's inspiration, personified as the son of that *belle nuit* which appeared in the first line. In both places there is the antithesis of darkness and light.

Then comes another invocation, with the urgent repetition of *Accours*, an invocation as if to a goddess known under many titles, a goddess of nature, source of the poet's genius, ruler of the world, finally named as *Uranie*, the Muse of Astronomy. The poet is not invoking the aid of a Muse of poetry, for the divinity his soul desires to commune with is the Muse whose domain is the whole natural universe. Another one-line sentence is here followed by a sentence of nine lines which flows from the constellations of Leo and Orion to the Milky Way. The strong *rejet* of the verb *Marchent* into line 16 follows this forceful movement. *L'astre du lion* is the most brilliant star of Leo (Regulus, a star of the first magnitude). *Les triples feux du superbe Orion* are the three stars of Orion's belt. Although the atmosphere of classical myth remains strong it is combined with the modernity of astronomical observation.

The movement then changes from the steady safety of *marchent* to the sinuous, uncontrolled flight of

> fugitive emporté,
> Tu suives les détours . . . (lines 17-18).

The Milky Way is evoked by a periphrasis which combines its true definition *soleils amoncelés,* with the explanation of its popular name,

Où le peuple a cru voir les traces d'un lait pur; (line 20)

and in which the colour and brightness of its appearance are emphasised: *voie argentée, soleils amoncelés, céleste azur, lait pur. Soleils amoncelés* also indicates its vastness.

The command *Accours* is repeated by *Descends* (line 21) which is similarly stressed by being placed at the beginning of the line. This command is however immediately amended: *non, porte-moi.* The poet himself desires to take flight among the celestial fires. The burning already suggested by *brûlant délire* (line 6) and *cheveux de flamme* (line 9) is added to here by *brûlante* and *flamme ardente,* to which attention is drawn by their being at the rhyme.

The poet has moved in this part of the passage, from the tranquil words addressed to night on the sea-shore, to the wish to become himself one of the heavenly fires.

In the second part this wish is fulfilled. There is no discontinuity between the two parts. The disembodied form of *flamme ardente* becomes his own when he is rid of his *corps pesant* (line 23). Bodily life, a tomb of flesh, is as death compared with his new freedom. Now weightless, he speeds through space, as Earth falls away beneath his feet. The short sentences and the monosyllables of line 25 help to convey this speed, as does the *rejet* of *M'aspire.* The word *éther* expresses the emptiness of space and *nage* has a fluid movement, confirmed and accentuated by the verb *aspirer,* which gives the impression of the effortlessness of the poet's upward movement, as if he were being drawn up by the breath of space. This fluidity appears again in *océan* and its endlessness in *sans rivage.*

Plus de nuit (line 27) is swift and marks the sudden realisation that earthly night is no more. The explanation is scientific, but its expression is poetic. Night occurs when the sun is on the other side of the globe of earth. In space there is no longer this barrier. The inversion of *d'un globe opaque et dur . . . l'impénétrable mur* places the wall at the end of the sentence, like a barrier, and the occlusive consonants of *globe opaque et dur* seem to express its solidity and hardness.

In line 29 *plus de nuit* is repeated, but this time in a longer, flowing sentence to convey the endless extent of time and space. The repeated structure of *et se perd et se mêle,* with its assonant verbs, backs up this effect. The floods of light in line 30 again have the image of fluidity in *torrents* and there seems to be an effective contrast between what Grammont would call the *voyelles graves* of *torrents profonds* and the *voyelles claires* of *lumière éternelle*, the latter giving an impression of lightness and clarity.

The poet then finds himself among the constellations, Cassiopeia, Ursa (the Great or the Little Bear), Delphinus, Corona Borealis (the Northern Crown), Aquila, Cygnus, Lyra, Pegasus and Serpens. Lyra may have been chosen because it suggests the poet's lyre, and Pegasus because the winged horse is sometimes used as a symbol of poetic inspiration. These ancient names, that the constellations still bear, are merely those given to them in human language. The poet exploits the poetic connotation of these names while suggesting that they do not convey the reality.

First of all the poet is *on* Cassiopeia, Ursa and Delphinus; the preposition *sur* has a curious precision. Then he is in the midst of the encircling Corona. Then comes an enumeration (line 34). The names are linked by the repeated *et* in a line which has no completed grammatical structure and thus adds to the impression of endless space. Then, further away still, comes the snake movement of

le Serpent tortueux
Noue autour de mes pas ses anneaux . . .

To these varied impressions of position, movement and shape are added the fire and brightness of *feu, s'embrase* and *lumineux*.

The poet next makes another apostrophe, not now to anything as imaginably tangible as Night or the Muse, but to space itself, whose immensity is fertile because it contains all that lives; its depths are *vivants*. For the poet the universe is not just a mechanism but something living, with which great souls (the souls of poets) have an affinity. Space is imagined as an abyss and the journey of the poetic soul as plunging into it.

An attempt can be made to analyse the harmony of lines 37 and 38, which seems to comprise several overlapping sound-patterns. The group [im] is heard in *immensité, magnanimes* and *abîme*. *Abîme* is repeated at the beginning of the next line (in terms of rhetoric, anadiplosis). This pattern is modulated by the syllable [ɛm] in *aiment* and emphasized by the fact that the rhyme *abîme/magnanime* also assonates in its penultimate syllables. There are additional [i] sounds in *immensité, esprits, vivants*. A second pattern is the chiasmus of the vowel [e] and [ɔ̃] in *féconde* and

1

plonger. Thirdly there is the pattern of the vowels [i] and [ã] in *immensité* and *vivants*. Of course no meaning can be attributed to these sound-patterns; there is simply a harmony which adds to the general poetic effect.

An abyss is generally conceived of as being dark. These, paradoxically, are *abîmes de clarté*. In this immensity man, freed of his earthly chains, is with, and becomes part of, the forces of creation. His soul, which by its poetry wished to commune with the gods (lines 10 and 11), has gone back to its origin (man was created in the image of God) and has once more become part of the divine essence.

The poet has moved from earthly darkness to eternal light. From images of night and the sea-shore he has progressed to a mystical experience, a pantheistic union with the universe.

It is necessary to remember to distinguish between the atheistic author of these lines and the poet to whom he attributes them. Chénier is not just describing an experience he has had. His poetic imagination has created both the experience and its expression. The plausibility of the experience depends on the effectiveness of the expression.

Chénier's skill with imagery shows in this fragment chiefly with images of movement and colour, or more precisely of brightness. His use of the alexandrine is classical, except in those *enjambements* and *rejets* which give a rhythm of speed or movement. While making use of the myths of antiquity, he is modern in his conception of the universe. He is very concerned with the sound of his poetry and some lines in this fragment look forward to the even denser sound-patterns of Mallarmé and Valéry.

This *morceau astronomique*, as Chénier called it, is highly lyrical, even though it was to be part of a poem which would have been mainly narrative and didactic.

M. J. O'R.

III

Charles Baudelaire, 1821-1867

Chant d'Automne

I

Bientôt nous plongerons dans les froides ténèbres;
Adieu, vive clarté de nos étés trop courts!
J'entends déjà tomber avec des chocs funèbres
4   Le bois retentissant sur le pavé des cours.

Tout l'hiver va rentrer dans mon être: colère,
Haine, frissons, horreur, labeur dur et forcé,
Et, comme le soleil dans son enfer polaire,
8   Mon cœur ne sera plus qu'un bloc rouge et glacé.

J'écoute en frémissant chaque bûche qui tombe;
L'échafaud qu'on bâtit n'a pas d'écho plus sourd.
Mon esprit est pareil à la tour qui succombe
12   Sous les coups du bélier infatigable et lourd.

Il me semble, bercé par ce choc monotone,
Qu'on cloue en grande hâte un cercueil quelque part.
Pour qui? – C'était hier l'été; voici l'automne!
16   Ce bruit mystérieux sonne comme un départ.

II

J'aime de vos longs yeux la lumière verdâtre,
Douce beauté, mais tout aujourd'hui m'est amer,
Et rien, ni votre amour, ni le boudoir, ni l'âtre,
20   Ne me vaut le soleil rayonnant sur la mer,

Et pourtant aimez-moi, tendre cœur! soyez mère,
Même pour un ingrat, même pour un méchant;
Amante ou sœur, soyez la douceur éphémère
24   D'un glorieux automne ou d'un soleil couchant.

Courte tâche! La tombe attend; elle est avide!
Ah! laissez-moi, mon front posé sur vos genoux,
Goûter, en regrettant l'été blanc et torride,
28   De l'arrière-saison le rayon jaune et doux!

(*Les Fleurs du Mal*)

Possible comparisons: 35, 49, 56

This poem was first published in *La Revue Contemporaine* of 30 November 1859, before appearing as poem no. 56 in the first section *Spleen et Idéal*, of the second edition of *Les Fleurs du Mal* (1861). It seems very probable that it was composed shortly before its publication.

The *Revue Contemporaine* version differed in three respects from the definitive version here printed: (a) lines 19 and 20 ran:

Et rien,même l'amour, la chambre étroite et l'âtre
Ne vaut l'ardent soleil rayonnant sur la mer.

– while (b) the poem bore the superscription "A M.D.", and (c) was not divided into two but printed as seven continuous stanzas. The first of these variants is not particularly important, though most readers would probably consider the definitive version preferable (*boudoir* falls within the same limits of literary convention as *âtre*, while *ardent* is not a particularly appropriate adjective for an autumn sun and thus produces an effect of padding). The "A M.D." almost certainly constitutes a dedication of the poem to the actress Marie Daubrun, but as our concern here is with the quality of the poem, not the poet's biography, this point is of minor relevance. The third variant indicates that in his initial conception the author saw the poem as a single unit whereas, initially at least, the definitive version may produce an effect of dichotomy. This is an aspect to which I shall refer in my conclusion.

The first line, with the downward movement suggested by *plongerons* and the association of *froides ténèbres* with dusk, autumn and death, contains resonances that are to be developed over the first three stanzas. *Etés trop courts* (I.2) makes the seasonal reference explicit and situates the poem at one level as a piece of realistic evocation: at the time it was written it was normal for families living in Paris to stock up in autumn with piles of logs for winter heating. But the adjective *funèbres* (I.3) already suggests a parallel between autumn and death, and this parallel is developed and strengthened in *échafaud* (I.10) and *cercueil* (I.14). The ideas associated with death, however, present it in more than just its physical reality: lines 5 and 6, with their enumeration of negative, joyless emotions (*colère, haine . . .*) make it clear that the poet is envisaging an atrophy of the will and the emotions that amounts to spiritual death (which is what he means by the *spleen* that provides one of the elements of the title of this section of *Les Fleurs du Mal*). The two ideas, of literal and metaphorical death, are powerfully combined in line 8, where on the one hand the ice-cold heart implies physical death, but the fact that the poet is conscious of this state gives the image metaphorical quality – the poet is telling us simultaneously of literal death and of a death-like inability to experience ordinary human feelings.

The first four stanzas are remarkable for the importance assumed throughout by the auditory image of the wood thudding onto the paved courtyards (II.3-4,9), which is extended to the imagined sound of hammering as the scaffold is built (I.10) or the coffin constructed (I.14), while the purely subjective experience of mental collapse is expressed by the analogous image of the battering-ram. In all these images there is the common element of the dull thudding sound – which is doubtless meant to suggest the thudding of the heart as awareness of approaching death is increasingly registered. Rhythms and sound patterns reflect the regularity and repetition of this sound image: of the first twelve lines, eleven are of regular, binary rhythm (the exception being I.5 which initiates the landscape-mood parallel), and such sound repetitions as that of the syllable [ɛr] in the second stanza (*hiver, colère, enfer, polaire*), or, more generally, of the veiled [r] sound (especially, but by no means exclusively, at the rhyme in all but the last of the poem's seven stanzas) are a reflection in sound of the statements being made. This feature is exemplified in masterly fashion in the open [p]'s four times occurring in succession in *choc monotone* (I.13).

In the first section the images have been urban and auditory, establishing in the reader's mind the figure of the poet, isolated, dejected and facing death in a city that is at best indifferent, at worst hostile. The second section centres on the feelings of the poet for a woman; death is still in prospect but is now used to give poignancy to the envisaged possibility of extracting a tranquil and largely nostalgic pleasure from the closing period of life. The opening image of the 'greenish' eyes (I.17) establishes the key for the imagery of this section, which is visual, relying principally on light and colour, especially the setting sun, which is evoked in the last line of each of the stanzas in this section. And whereas movement in the first four stanzas had been almost exclusively downward (*plonger, tomber, succomber*) horizontality here becomes a key feature (*longs yeux*, setting sun). Another noteworthy feature here is the relatively greater importance of abstract terms compared with those found in Section I; and whereas the latter are uniformly unpleasant or menacing (I.5-6), the emphasis in Section II, despite *amer, ingrat, méchant* II.18-22), is on a gentle tenderness (*douce beauté, tendre cœur, douceur, goûter, regretter*).

The rhythms in the last three stanzas are very different, too, from those of the first three, already mentioned as being regular. Fewer than half the lines are binary, 'regular' alexandrines (only II.17,20,22,24,28 are binary). In the others, the caesura is displaced (e.g. the main pause in II.18 occurs after the fourth syllable, in II.19 after the second, in II.21 after the ninth), and in one case the line is a 'ternary', with two equal pauses (II.25: *Courte tâch/e! ·La tombe attend; / elle est avide!*). These more complex rhythms are both a reinforcement and a reflection of the more complex sentence structures of Section II. The diction becomes more 'poetic' in the conventional – but not pejorative – sense (cf. the inversions of II.17 – *de vos longs yeux* – and II.28 – *De l'arrière-saison* – as well as the vocabulary already noted); accumulation (II.19: *ni . . . ni . . . ni . . .*), repetition (II.21.23: *soyez mère . . . soyez la douceur . . .*) and rich rhyme (*amer . . . l/a mer; soy/ez mère . . . éph/ émère*) are other examples of this contrast. Euphony is at least as evident as in Section I: cf. the *cœur, sœur, douceur* internal rhyme in stanza 6.

A further – and subtler – element in the change of mood is the rhythm, at once more complex and more ample. Several of the lines in Section I contain complete sentences (I.1, 2, 9, 10, 15, 16); it is true that there is a very close parallel in rhythmic and structural pattern between lines 15 and 25, but apart from the latter line the syntax of the sentences in the last three stanzas occupies, or comes near to occupying, the whole stanza. In stanza 6, for instance, the repetition of syntactic elements in a kind of diffused anaphora cements what would otherwise be separate sentences into a stylistic unit expressing a crescendo of yearning (*aimez-moi . . . soyez . . . soyez; même pour . . . même pour; Amante ou sœur . . . automne ou . . . soleil*). The longest sentence in the poem is the concluding one, and here the rhythm reaches its broadest and slowest: by distributing the three basic grammatical elements of the sentence over each of the last three lines (*laissez-moi . . . goûter . . . le rayon*) the poet ensures that these lines are spoken as a single unit; by the adverbial phrase of II.26 (*mon front posé sur vos genoux*), the participial clause of II.27 (*en regrettant l'été*) and the inversion of II.28 (*De l'arrière-saison le rayon*) he ensures that the line is spoken with a number of strongly marked pauses, and this slowing of the line is further emphasised by the fact that there are five stressed syllables in each of these lines:

> *Ah*! laissez-*moi*, mon *front* posé sur vos *genoux*,
> Goû*ter*, en regret*tant* l'é*té blanc* et tor*ride*,
> De l'arrière-sai*son* le ra*yon jaune* et *doux*.

(whereas four stresses per line is the commonest number found in the alexandrine). This *rallentando*, slowing of the pace, helps to establish the atmosphere of tranquillity that contrasts so sharply with the broken rhythms of line 25, and contributes in such a marked degree to a resolution of the antithesis between recollection of happiness and apprehension of death, informing as it does the close of the poem with a feeling of acceptance.

The contrast between sections I and II is further heightened by a whole series of antitheses. Autumn in Section I is seen as the prelude to winter, thus cold is stressed, whereas in Section II it is conceived as an extension of summer and is therefore warm (*le soleil, la douceur, l'été torride, le rayon doux*). The city, full of people busy with their own affairs, fades away, to give place to the calm seashore and a single, tender companion. Similarly, whereas autumn is first presented as the brief prelude to death, it is then shown as the bitter-sweet prolongation of life's summer.

Put in these terms, and with the poem unequivocally divided by Baudelaire, it could seem that the work lacks unity. That it does in fact come across to the reader as a unified whole seems to me to be explained by the nature of the fourth and seventh stanzas, that is the stanzas that complete each part of the poem.

In the case of stanza four there are two elements to be taken into account. By its subject matter, at any rate on the surface, it belongs where Baudelaire has put it, in Section I: the poet is still alone among his fellow city-dwellers, assailed by fears of darkness, winter and death. But there are two features that serve to detach it from the preceding stanzas. The first concerns rhythm: eleven of the first twelve lines have been rhythmically regular, that is with a marked caesura in the middle of the line (the dislocation in line 5 has not been violent - though by bringing *colère* into close association with *haine* etc. it has the effect of highlighting the change of emphasis from the world outside to that of the poet's mind). Compared with the regularity of the first three stanzas, the rhythmic irregularities of the fourth, in lines 13 and 15 (the main pause occurring after three and two syllables respectively) are much more disruptive: they alert the attentive reader to the fact that a shift of emphasis is taking place. Rhythmically, the poet is anticipating the much freer rhythms of Section II. But there is a second important feature of this stanza: despite the apparent continuation of the theme as already handled, a significant development is effected in lines 15 and 16. There is first of all the question *Pour qui?* This question is not simply rhetorical, in the sense that the answer is obvious. We assume of course that the coffin is being prepared for the poet; but by now, we are firmly established in the domain of metaphor and the imagination. The world of the wood-merchant and the everyday has been supplanted, so that the 'summer' and 'autumn' of the rest of this line are no longer the seasons of the year, but elements of the poet's life. This means that the departure evoked in line 16 is the setting out on the sea of death. (This line is almost a condensation of the theme of *Le Voyage*, the final poem in the collection that forms a comprehensive epilogue to *Les Fleurs du Mal*, summing up in a masterly way the complex themes of the work and – significantly – written a few months before the likely date of composition of *Chant d'Automne*).

Finally, although it is true that the last stanza has the overall effect of concentrating attention on such emotions as tranquillity, resigned acceptance and attempted oblivion of the future, it nevertheless brings together the three time levels of the poem. *L'été blanc et torride* of line 27 is an echo of *nos étés trop courts* of line 2, and through the feeling of regretfulness that it engenders it unites the present with the past. On the other hand, the brief recognition of *La tombe attend* (II.25) brings the element of impending threat – which is the substance of Section I – into immediate relation also with the present. So the poet builds up to a satisfactory climax in which the present is valued for the precarious balance it holds between an evanescent past and a doom-laden future. The poem succeeds by giving permanent form to a transient interplay of moods.

S.W.T.

IV

Henri Michaux, 1899–1984

Dans la Nuit

Dans la nuit
Dans la nuit
Je me suis uni à la nuit
A la nuit sans limites
5   A la nuit

Mienne, belle, mienne

Nuit
Nuit de naissance
Qui m'emplit de mon cri
10   De mes épis.
Toi qui m'envahis
Qui fais houle houle
Qui fais houle tout autour
Et fumes, es fort dense
15   Et mugis
Es la nuit.
Nuit qui gît, nuit implacable
Et sa fanfare, et sa plage
Sa plage en haut, sa plage partout,
20   Sa plage boit, son poids est roi, et tout ploie sous lui
Sous lui, sous plus ténu qu'un fil
Sous la nuit
La Nuit.

(*Un Certain Plume*)

©Editions Gallimard

Possible comparisons: 58, 78

    La nuit, contrairement à ce que je croyais, est plus multiple que le jour . . . (1). In *Dans la nuit* (1937) night is presented not only as *multiple*, but also to some extent as a *gouffre profond* (2). We need then to explore beyond the superficial, exorcistic level of the poem in order to come to grips with its total magic thought. 'Magic thought', as opposed to 'logical thought', is the contrast to which Michaux refers in the following lines from Postface: *Gardons-nous de suivre la pensée d'un auteur* . . . , *regardons plutôt ce qu'il a derrière la tête* (my underlining),

(1) H. Michaux, *Au Pays de la Magic*, 1941
(2) H. Michaux, *La Nuit remue*, 1935

où il veut en venir, l'empreinte que son désir de domination et d'influence, quoique bien caché, essaie de nous imposer. 'Behind the head', so wide is the potential of *Dans la Nuit* that it is clearly inappropriate to speak of the poem's one, final, clear-cut meaning or message, no matter how exorcistic or magical. It may indeed be the case that the poem's apparent simplicity (*is* it about 'night'?) overlays various complementary textures of evocation. Our personal reactions to these may well lead us to our individual 'Land of Magic' . . .

In lines 1-5, abstract *nuit* gains almost a tangible quality by its repetition five times in as many lines. By line 3, the incantatory tone is already established, since lines 1 and 2 are of course identical to the title. Yet *Dans la Nuit* (title, plus lines 1 and 2) forms the framework within which is situated the phrase *à la nuit* (occurring three times in lines 3-5) with its more sharply-focused preposition *à*. Expert at paradox, Michaux opposes the idea of confinement, conveyed by the triple *dans* of *dans la nuit*, to the boundless notion of *la nuit sans limites* (line 4). With a similar antithetical gesture, the idea of *presence*, implied by *dans la nuit*, is juxtaposed to the idea of *absence* conveyed by *sans limites*, the former phrase containing a positive and the latter a negative overtone. Note that *Je* is poised at the beginning of line 3 at the centre of this night, which, as we have just seen, is at once limited and limitless. The syntax confirms the central, – even cosy – position of *Je*, protected on the one side by its reflexive pronoun, yet on the other intriguingly vulnerable to its abstract complement *à la nuit! Je* is, as it were, cocooned by night, but on the brink of the unknown. Just as the subject, *Je* is contained within the reflexive nature of the construction, so, in a kind of parallel way, does *nuit* in lines 1,2,4 and 5 encompass the main clause of line 3 to create the impression of layers within layers. In other words, general, boundless night, its emptiness reinforced by the lack of adjectival support for *nuit*, envelops even the more specific night of *à la nuit* (line 3) at the centre of which is the subject, *Je*. Alternatively, the inner space, *l'espace du dedans* is contained within the outer space, *l'espace du dehors*.

So, at the risk of labouring the point, the pivot and the subject of lines 1-5 is the *Je* of line 3! Despite the lack of punctuation, the grammatical sequence of lines 1-5 is quite unambiguous. The perfect tense of line 3, *Je me suis uni*, indicates a present, static finality, contrasting markedly with the subsequent use of tenses.

In *La Nuit remue*, Michaux writes: *Sous le plafond bas de ma petite chambre, est ma nuit, gouffre profond.* (My emphasis). Line 6 of *Dans la Nuit* contains a similar idea: the poet's (and by this stage the reader's also) personal possession of an abstract, natural occurrence – the positive, personal possession of negative night with its absence of light.

To this idea of the positive possession of absence is added the incongruous *belle* (line 6), which retrospectively throws a fresh light on line 3, *Je me suis uni à la nuit*. It is obvious that Michaux is, so to speak, in love with the beautiful night, albeit that the adjective *belle* qualifying *nuit* affords meagre purchase for our imagination. However, the enveloping void has been transformed into an animate, almost personified night, with limitless possibilities, despite the fact that Michaux has as yet used no more than 21 words! The static construction of lines 1-5 contrasts with the overall development of the poet's feeling, especially when line 6 is taken into consideration.

Our initial impression in lines 1-5 of a void, empty apart from *Je*, is shown in lines 7-20 to have been premature. Here, quite fascinatingly, the void – or night – exists in various dimensions of time and space. Night now undergoes considerable shape-shifting and development, as a consequence of which the *Je* of line 3 assumes a less prominent role, although of course its sense is kept alive by the repeated pronoun *me* (lines 9 and 11) and possessive adjectives *mon* (line 9) and *mes* (line 10). Emphasis now turns towards the poet's personal reactions to those areas of his sensitivity which are triggered by the subject of night. Line 7 opens almost with an apostrophe to *Nuit*, although the tone of the address is perhaps more explicitly conveyed by the repetition of *Nuit* in *Nuit de naissance* (line 8). We are now in a position to confirm the impression gained in line 6 that for Michaux night has a human overtone. An immediate contrast is thus apparent between the objective *nuit sans limites* of line 4, as yet unresponsive to the subject of lines 1-5 and the direct appeal to a night with more intimate connotations in *Nuit de naissance* (line 8). Certainly, by this stage in the poem, the unevenly-placed repetition of *nuit* has caught our attention; furthermore, the sparse, economical means of expression in lines 1-6 serves only to enhance our sense of expectation.

The idea of the union of the poet with night is first mentioned in line 3; to this idea is added, as we have seen, the personal, possessive aspect in line 6. Whereas in these earlier lines the focal point, the subject of the construction is the *Je* of line 3, the focus from line 7 onwards is on *Nuit*, from which radiate in lines 9 and 11-15 a number of apparently disconnected relative clauses. The fact that the subject, *Nuit* is not restated in lines 9-15, indeed, enhances the force of *Nuit* in lines 7 and 8, which stand now – as we cast our eye back – at the head of a series of note-form comments. Yet, by contrast with the non-repetition of *Nuit*, the relative *qui* is carefully repeated in lines 9, 11, 12 and 13, after which, in lines 14-16, it temporarily vanishes. The lack of repetition of *Nuit* in 9-15 is given a further slant by virtue of its contrast with the five instances of *nuit* in lines 1-5.

lx

Whereas in lines 1-5 Michaux is stretching out to night, treating it as an *entity*, from line 7 onwards the roles are varied to the extent that here (lines 7-10) Michaux becomes, so to speak, the observer at his own birth. Furthermore, line 9 introduces the first reference in the poem to sound, making us aware, as we look back, of the airless, soundless quality of lines 1-6, – as if poet and reader hold their breath on the verge of some magical awareness. The *real* world on which Michaux's imaginary journey is based is not hard to find. Yet Michaux characteristically fuses the real with the poetic world by use of the symbolic *nuit*, which in a paradoxical way, combines the notion of abstract nothingness with that of a womb from which he is born – and born to live (*mon cri*, line 9). If the cadence of line 5 suggests to us that night represents a goal achieved by the poet, then line 7 onwards shows us the obverse: that night is the very beginning of the poet's world. Again, the real element, the fact that as we see it, day emerges from night, is not obscure! But the basic elements of reality are transformed by Michaux into a new world in which magic is the predominant force.

The magically creative power of night does not stop at *filling the poet with his first cry* (see line 9). Rather does the logic of idea-association lead Michaux to *épis* (line 10) – a particularly evocative visual image with many associations of which the most significant here is the continuation of the life-giving force. Despite the free-flowing effect created by the lack of punctuation, line 11 shows us the poet's mind darting in yet another direction. His birth and invigoration come from night; in these lines (7-10) he addresses night and yet at the same time stands beside himself as an observer. However, in one sense line 11 is independent from what precedes. Michaux is overwhelmed by night in line 11, but in another sense this line extends the idea of lines 7-10 that night is the source of life-force.

So far, the poem has hardly impinged on us visually; indeed, if we discount the colours implicit in idea-association, the multiple *épis* (line 10) is the only visual image. Lines 12 and 13, however, invite us to associate by implication the surge of the night (*nuit* being the subject of these lines) with the ebb and flow of the sea, its endless rolling evoked by the thrice repeated *houle* in these lines, with a further echo of the surge contained in the assonance of *tout autour* (line 13). Perhaps note in addition the implied sound of *hou* (hoot) contained within that of *houle*. Yet whereas in the visual, superficial sense we may think of the sea as two-dimensional, in line 13 night is presented in three dimensions: it surges *tout autour*. Night, then, is within (line 11) and also without (line 13); moreover, external night may be sensed by means other than visual in its tactile density (*dense*, line 14). Its smoky, misty quality (*fumes*, line 14) makes it tangible and oppressive. The cry given by Michaux in line 9 (*mon cri*), the sound generated by night and which proves that life exists, is now matched in line 15, *Et mugis* – that is to say by the roar/moan made by night as it surges like the sea. *Mon cri* (line 9) and *mugis* (line 15) refer to the same life-force, but at the same time extend the parallel between internal reality (*mon cri*) and external reality (the roar of night). The vital surge of lines 7–15 relapses into the static idea conveyed by line 16 with its fixed 1:1 quality: (*Nuit*) [tu] *Es la nuit*, but which reminds us that lines 7–17 are in the form of an address to night. In fact this static note is maintained from line 17 to the end of the poem and is effectively stressed by the tomb-like monosyllables of line 17: *Nuit qui gît*. Here Michaux is no longer addressing night, but rather is commenting, again as an observer, on the recumbent quality of personified night, which has remained detached from the poet despite his address in lines 7–16. Yet, *implacable* (line 17) though it may be, it is this same night – perhaps at several removes – with which Michaux enjoyed the intimacy expressed in lines 1–6 and which filled him with life and vigour in lines 7–16.

Suddenly, lines 18–23 take us in a different direction where night, it appears, is conceived as a vast, heavy *plage*, suffocating everything beneath it. Here is an example of the shape-shifting alluded to above, for no sooner have we absorbed line 20, which is an intentionally cumbersome, overblown, tripartite *alexandrine*, than we find ourselves confronted with the notion that night is stretched taut like a string. Only a moment earlier, night was so inflated (line 20) that it dominated its beach in a menacing way. Thus the abstract *nuit* of line 1 has been transformed into gigantic, personified *Nuit implacable* of line 17, whose weight asphyxiates everything (line 20), and whose personification is emphasised by the monosyllable *Nuit*, the last word in the poem.

The thematic development of the poem is fascinating: lines 1–6 introduce us to the poet's unsuspecting, possessive relationship with night; in lines 7–16 we find that night becomes associated with life; the last seven lines of the poem show how, for Michaux, night brings no permanent comfort, indeed no permanent life. So we may see in this a transition from optimism to a condition of resignation, almost of despair. Michaux's incantation accordingly takes on a serious note – that of a desperate cry for release from a force which seems paradoxically to be at once that of life and of death. It is entirely in keeping with his outlook that Michaux should feel intoxicated (lines 1–6) with that from which he knows no escape and which will annihilate him (the final lines of the poem).

If we now briefly examine the form and the sound of the poem, we shall see that its poetic effects are largely created by the masterly accumulation of assonance and alliteration. The effectiveness of these devices is enhanced by the fact that since the lines are not isometric it is not possible to detect a definite rhythm-pattern. In this kind of free-verse, it is sense-rhythms which condition both the line-lengths and the frequency with which poetic devices occur. Furthermore, internal rhyme, assonance and repetition play a crucial role in the creation of the incantatory effect. These various factors – and particularly the varying line-lengths – give the poem its spontaneous quality.

Now for a closer look at some of these points: lines 1-5 take the form of a musical phrase which widens *crescendo* to the the centre of line 3, after which the lines move towards the cadence of line 5. To continue the musical analogy, lines 1 and 2 constitute in effect a repeated bar (incidentally repeating without alteration the 'theme' announced in the title) which introduces the theme of union with night, after which the longer third and fourth lines represent the development of the expressive crescendo–decrescendo and add an important detail before reaching the subtle cadence of line 5. The key does not change in lines 1-5, yet the harmony of line 5 (*A (la nuit)*) introduces a note which is delicately different from that of the title and of lines 1 and 2 (*dans (la nuit)*). The overall musical effect of these lines is, however, only partially a function of their construction. To this is added the sonority created specifically by the repetition of the [n] sounds. A further point is that the lines are underpinned by a remarkably narrow vocalic range: in 21 words (i.e. lines 1-5), the vowel [a] occurs eight times. As we have already agreed, however, the disposition of sounds is conditioned by the sense-rhythms so that a regular, monotonous, vocalic effect is avoided. Among other recurring sounds (evocative of exorcism) are the nasal [ã] in *dans* (lines 1 and 2, and *sans* (line 4); [ɥi] occurs five times in *nuit* and once in *suis* (line 3). Particularly effective is the initial [n] of the five-times repeated *nuit*, coupled with the alliterative bonus of *uni* (line 3). Yet despite the concentrated repetitive devices of lines 1-5, we note that, with the exception of the full stop at the end of line 5, the lines gain fluidity from their lack of punctuation.

Sparse punctuation continues to be a characteristic of the rest of the poem, as does also the extension of the assonance and alliteration already established in lines 1-5. The use of repeated sounds *within* certain lines must also be stressed, as, for example, in lines 7 and 8, where the [n] of repeated *nuit* is carried on into *naissance*. The five-times repeated [m] of lines 9-11 forms a *block* of sound, taken up again in lines 14, *fumes* and 15, *mugis*. The cumulative effect of line 9, *empli, cri,* line 10 *épis,* line 11, *qui m'envahis,* lines 12 and 13, *qui,* line 15, *mugis,* and line 17, *qui gît* is hypnotic. Retrospectively it becomes all the more potent on account of the absence of this [i] sound in lines 18-20. The beginnings of each line illustrate Michaux's use of individual words which are in themselves simple, but which take on added force when grouped in a more concentrated way: lines 1 and 2: *Dans*; lines 4 and 5: *A*; lines 7 and 8: *Nuit*; lines 12 and 13: *Qui*; lines 14 and 15: *Et*; lines 19 and 20: *Sa*; lines 21 and 22: *Sous*. This type of repetition, contributing as it does to the hallucinatory effect, means that the poem's 23 lines begin with only 13 different words, all of which (with the exception of *Mienne*, (line 6) are distinct monosyllables. By virtue of their concentrated simplicity they help to call forth the atmosphere of a chant.

In *La Nuit remue* Michaux write: *La nuit venue, ma chambre silencieuse se remplit de monde et de bruits . . .* Our poem illustrates the verbal journey made by the poet from the starting point of reality through the imagination and subsequently back to a transformed reality. The main purpose of this journey appears to be the creation of a special kind of magical awareness and the exploration of the boundaries between imagination and reality. As we have noted, these effects are in no way achieved by unusual vocabulary, but rather by simple, concise statements of which the hallmark is several types of repetition. Thus sound-patterns take on a musical, non-verbal significance over and above the literal or even poetic meanings of the constructions. It is not easy to remain impervious to the hypnotic spell created by these sound-patterns; indeed it is poetically most rewarding and satisfying to investigate the different levels which come to the surface on each fresh reading.

J.M.D.

Honorat Laugier de Porchères, 1572-1653

Sur les Yeux de
Madame la Duchesse de Beaufort

Ce ne sont pas des yeux, ce sont plutôt des dieux,
Ils ont dessus les rois la puissance absolue;
Dieux, non, ce sont des cieux, ils ont la couleur bleue,
4   Et le mouvement prompt comme celui des cieux.

Cieux, non, mais deux soleils clairement radieux
Dont les rayons brillants nous offusquent la vue;
Soleils, non, mais éclairs de puissance inconnue,
8   Des foudres de l'amour signes présagieux.

Car s'ils étaient des dieux feraient-ils tant de mal?
Si des cieux, ils auraient leur mouvement égal;
Deux soleils, ne se peut: le soleil est unique.

12   Eclairs, non: car ceux-ci durent trop et trop clairs.
Toutefois je les nomme, afin que je m'explique,
Des yeux, des dieux, des cieux, des soleils, des éclairs.

(1597)

Paul Eluard, 1895-1952

"La courbe de tes yeux"

La courbe de tes yeux fait le tour de mon cœur,
Un rond de danse et de douceur,
Auréole du temps, berceau nocturne et sûr,
Et si je ne sais plus tout ce que j'ai vécu,
5   C'est que tes yeux ne m'ont pas toujours vu.

Feuilles de jour et mousse de rosée,
Roseaux du vent, sourires parfumés,
Ailes couvrant le monde de lumière,
Bateaux chargés du ciel et de la mer,
10   Chasseurs des bruits et sources des couleurs,

Parfums éclos d'une couvée d'aurores,
Qui gît toujours sur la paille des astres,
Comme le jour dépend de l'innocence
Le monde entier dépend de tes yeux purs
15   Et tout mon sang coule dans leurs regards.

Capitale de la douleur

© Editions Gallimard

Possible comparisons: 58, 60, 71, 73

These two poems, written more than three centuries apart, have obvious common factors in subject-matter (a woman's eyes), its treatment (by means of metaphor) and in scale; moreover, both poems have a fairly closely-knit structure, although the details of the structure differ. A detailed analysis of the two poems will bring out the major differences between them, and perhaps also further similarities that are not apparent at a first reading. The structural patterns are too dissimilar for the poems to be successfully analysed in parallel (as one can, on occasion analyse in parallel two sonnets, comparing quatrains with quatrains and tercets with tercets), so the appropriate procedure is to start with a straight-forward exposition of the earlier poem, with which the second can subsequently be compared.

Porchères's poem takes as its subject the eyes of Gabrielle d'Estrées, mistress of the French King Henri IV; its technical brilliance is in part a reflection of its status as a court poem. In terms of external structure it conforms to the traditional pattern of the sonnet, established as the standard form for short lyric poems by the Italian poet Petrarch in the mid-14th century, and introduced into France in the early 16th century. The two four line stanzas (quatrains) have *rimes embrassées*; the tercets, rhyming *ccd ede* adopt one of the less rigid of the various schemes permissible, using three rhymes rather than two. The rhymes themselves are not particularly obtrusive; only one (*clairs / éclairs*) is *riche*, the remainder being *suffisantes*, or, in the case of *absolue / bleue / vue / inconnue , pauvres*. (In the late sixteenth century *eu* could still be a genuine diphthong (two sounds) so rhymes between *bleue* and other words ending in *-ue*, which would not be permissible in modern French were permissible then). However, these relatively weak rhymes are underpinned by other structural elements, as will be seen later, and the lines are so securely end-stopped that there is no danger of the unity of the alexandrine being undermined; although there are cases where the strongest break in the line is not the regular caesura (e.g. lines 10 and 12), this is not associated with enjambement, and the lines remain intact, if somewhat disjointed.

The organisation of the material in the sonnet follows a pattern that is typical of the sonnet form, though by no means universal: the quatrains are used to present a proposition, evoke a situation, or, as here, develop an image or series of images, which gives rise to a comment or reflection in the tercets. The break after the quatrains marks a change of rhymes, a change of rhythm (from four-line to three-line units), and a change of tone. In this poem, however, there is some divergence from an exact harmony of internal and external structure, for, as we shall see later, the argument of the tercets suggests a division into a four line group followed by a couplet rather than into two groups of three lines.

Within the quatrains, the pattern is one of rigid parallelism; after the initial dismissal of the literal reality of the eyes with *Ce ne sont pas des yeux*, four successive metaphors are introduced (*ce sont plutôt des dieux* etc.), justified (*ils ont dessus les rois*, etc.), and finally rejected (*Dieux, non*). This last element is the most unusual aspect of the presentation of the metaphors in this poem: it is commonplace for metaphors relating to a single object to follow each other in a sequence, in which each is superimposed on the one before, but much less common for one metaphor to be explicitly replaced by another. The tercets of the poem emphasise this distinctive negative approach, providing almost a mirror-image of the quatrains, where the link between the metaphorical word and the reality it represents (the *vehicle* and the *tenor* of the metaphor, to use the terminology provided by I. A. Richards), is explained, and the negation of this link is expressed in the single word *non*. Now the *negation* is explained, with one line to each metaphor (lines 9-12); in the two final lines the poet completes his tour de force by asserting that all five labels, the literal term *yeux* and its four metaphorical equivalents, are all valid. Here the discrepancy between internal and external structures becomes apparent: the argument links line 12 with the preceding tercet, leaving lines 13-14 as a two line conclusion. (This pattern, for which there are precedents in Petrarch, is relatively common in both Italian and French poets; in some English sonnets it rapidly became the norm, and the rhyme-scheme was modified to produce the so-called *Shakespearean* sonnet, composed of three quatrains and a rhyming couplet).

Closer examination of the way the metaphors are presented shows a close parallelism in syntax between the two halves of each quatrain. In the first quatrain the two new images are introduced, after the rejection of the previous one, by *ce sont*, contrasting with the initial *Ce ne sont pas*, and establishing the verb *être* as the dominant verb of the whole poem – a poem in which the successive metaphors are explicitly presented not as indicators of a series of different but compatible aspects of the subject, but as mutually exclusive elements in a frustrating attempt at definition. The problem they suggest is not how reality appears, but what it is. The explanations of each metaphor in this first quatrain are also parallel: attributes of each image are introduced by *ils sont*, with no subordinating conjunction to make the relationship between the clauses explicit. It is perfectly clear that the two *ils sont* clauses *explain* the images that precede them; the absence of *puisque* or other causal conjuction makes for a more condensed and forceful argument. The parallelism is reinforced by the rhyme of *yeux, dieux* and *cieux* which links the literal term to the two metaphors within the lines, as well as providing the outer pair of rhymes in the formal rhyme-scheme. These various parallelisms, however, are not so rigid as to make this first quatrain a purely mechanical structure: the opening hemistich serves to displace the first metaphor, so that this is introduced in the latter half of line 1, whereas the second metaphor, *cieux*, appears in the *first* half of line 3.

As for the metaphors themselves, what is their significance in this attempt to pin down the reality of the eyes? The first image is conventional in its origin, and its justification is a witty reminder of the context of the poem, for the king's infatuation with the subject of the poem would be well known to its first readers. The second metaphor is rather less conventional, and there is a contrast in the atmosphere suggested by the metaphor *dieux*, emphasising the emotional power of eyes, and that of *cieux*, underlining their physical appearance and behaviour – though both images suggest the idea of absolute perfection.

In the second quatrain the parallelism of structure is closer, with no introductory phrase to displace the first metaphor: each metaphor is introduced in exactly the same way and appears at the same point in the line. There is, however, a difference between the two descriptive developments, the first being a relative clause (line 6), and the second a phrase in apposition (*signes présagieux*). This time there is no internal rhyme to provide an obvious 'cross-referencing' effect; the rhyming words, *radieux* and *présagieux* emphasise significant aspects of each metaphor, and of course provide an echo of the preceding quatrain, but they are not the focus of the argument. The assonance between *clairement* and *éclairs* perhaps serves to bind the two images together to some extent, for although the two words are different parts of speech, a factor which would tend to work against a close association in the reader's mind, this is partly offset by the fact that the common derivation of the two words is still perceptible in their meanings. These two new images, both of them familiar and clearly explained, are developed in a way that reinforces the sense of perplexity: the first builds up a vision not only of brilliance (*radieux, rayons brillants*) but also of clarity (*clairement*), only to upset it with the paradoxical *offusquent la vue* – not an entirely new idea, but one that is given a new vigour by the choice of the verb *offusquer*, with its explicit suggestion of darkness, rather than the conventional *éblouir*. The lightning flashes (*éclairs*) are the traditional example of light that blinds by its very brilliance, so the second metaphor of the quatrain follows logically from the first; whereas in the first quatrain the principal connection between the two metaphors is verbal, or, more strictly, phonetic, in this case the connection is one of meaning. The power of the lightning echoes the power of the gods (repetition of *puissance*), though the different adjectives (*absolue, inconnue*) reflect the shift from dogmatic certainty in the first quatrain to paradox and uncertainty in the second. Finally, we are reminded that all these attempts to define the eyes in terms of various superhuman forces are to be seen in the context of a love poem; we must not lose sight of the poem's basic function as a poem in praise of a royal mistress, even though the pattern of argument may suggest deeper problems beneath the courtly subject-matter.

Up to this point, the poem has moved forward on the principle of *reculer pour mieux sauter*: each new image is justified by the poet, and seems to represent an advance on the previous one that has just been dismissed. But now, in lines 9-12, the poet goes through all the *negative* arguments, the reasons why each image in turn is unsatisfactory. The condensed, sometimes elliptical expression becomes even more marked, as if a professor of logic or a fictional detective were going through his notes on a possible solution to his problem and eliminating each one in turn. The whole process implies a confrontation between two incompatible ways of looking at reality, the poet's use of metaphor in which *one* significant similarity between tenor and vehicle is sufficient to warrant an assertion of identity, and the scientist or logician's search for a water-tight definition, in which *all* the elements must correspond. By the end of line 12 the logician has destroyed the elaborate edifice whose weakness the poet had already pointed out, leaving the poet to re-erect it with a defiant gesture in the closing lines of the poem. The logician has shown that the eyes can be neither gods, skies, suns, nor flashes of lightning; but the poet asserts that for him they are all four, without ceasing to be themselves. The first-person verbs *je les nomme, je m'explique* perhaps suggest that our grasp of reality is something personal, transcending the generalising faculty of logic or common sense; but the over-riding impression left by the poem is of an awareness that reality is complex, and perhaps in the end undefinable. Despite the neat way in which the poet asserts that *all* the metaphors are valid, the conclusion rings hollow, and the forcefulness of the negatives in the poem leaves us with the feeling that the technical *tour de force* has simply brought us round in a circle, that reality is too uncertain and unstable to be grasped at all.

–: –: –: –: –: –

Eluard's poem is presumed to have been inspired by his first wife, Gala, but it carries no title that might limit its reference; although the initial *tutoiement* and the use of the first person in the opening line implies a personal experience, it is a personal experience that may be shared – very different from Porchères's sonnet, where the *je* who appears at the end of the poem is the poet-craftsman, the manipulator of ideas rather than the feeling and imagining human being. Eluard does not follow a strict form laid down in advance, although his poem has a clearly discernible pattern (three stanzas of five lines each), with rhyme used in an apparently random manner, as is the variation of line-lengths in the first stanza. This first stanza gives a deceptive impression of the form of the poem, in that it does not provide the pattern for the other two, as would be the case in *regular* stanzaic verse. It shows a rhyme scheme of sorts, which we could denote *aab* (*cc*): the *c* rhyme is only a *rime pauvre*, but it assonates with the otherwise isolated third line. This pattern does not recur in the following stanzas: the second stanza has assonances between lines 6 and 7, 8 and 9, whereas in the final stanza the only trace of phonetic identity between line endings is the very weak *aurores* / *astres*. So rhyme, which at first sight looks like being a significant formal element, progressively evaporates during the course of the poem.

The situation is reversed when we look at the structure of the lines: after the 12. 8. 12. 12. 10 of the first stanza, the remaining two stanzas settle into regular decasyllabic lines, with the metrical break after the fourth syllable in every case. The rhymes, which help to establish the unity of the lines in the first stanza, are less necessary in the metrically regular stanzas that follow. In other respects, the verse follows the traditional rules, with *mute e's* counting as syllables; the only exception is *couvée* in line 11, which would not be acceptable in orthodox versification.

The internal structure of the poem partly harmonises with this division into three stanzas, partly conflicts with it: the second stanza begins a new sentence, a new *movement*, but this then continues without any *logical* break until the end of the poem. The question arises whether the gap on the printed page between stanzas two and three is purely arbitary, or an invitation to the reader to pause and perhaps adjust to a change of mood, even though there is no break in the syntax. The theme of the eyes and their power is introduced directly in the first line, and the reader is immediately drawn into the poet's world through the possessives *tes* and *mon*, in contrast with the forceful negative by which Porchères seems to challenge the reader's perception of reality. But Eluard questions or undermines our preconceptions no less effectively than Porchères, for although he gives us no explicit signposts as to the novelty of his imagery, the phrases he uses to convey the effect of the eyes on his emotions and imagination are far from everyday expressions. Where Porchères appeals to the intellect, Eluard writes with his imagination, and in order to appreciate his poem each individual reader must involve his own imagination: no two readings of the poem will be identical, and each will involve some degree of creative activity.

The opening image immediately transcends the plane of literal description, for what is *La courbe de tes yeux*? We have a vision of a sweeping curve that extends to encompass the poet's heart – an intensely visual way of expressing the link between eyes and emotions, that Porchères conveyed in a much more abstract way with images whose connotations were relatively fixed, so that his reader's reactions to them could be fairly accurately predicted. But visual though it is, we cannot readily *visualise* Eluard's image, without rejecting, or at least modifying our everyday vision of reality. It is not simply a concrete metaphor expressing an abstract reality, a parallel between two distinct planes, but a total fusion of the two. The assonance between *courbe* and *tour* reinforces the association between these two metaphorical terms, each taking the emphasis in the first half of their hemistich, as the literal terms *yeux* and *cœur* take the emphasis at the end; this effect of symmetry strengthens the impact of the initial statement, which the remainder of the poem goes on to elaborate. The image of the curve or circle is taken up again in the second line, where it is developed by two images which make the emotional atmosphere more specific – the active, joyful *danse* (which can easily be visualised as a circle), and the passive *douceur*. These two images seem disparate, but they are brought together as complementary aspects of the same mood by a combination of phonetic and syntactic links: alliteration, and the grammatical structure which places them both in the same relation to *Un rond de*. The presence of the article *Un* implies that this line forms an additional object for the verb *fait*, whereas the following phrases, without articles, stand in apposition to a noun, presumably *rond*.

In line 3 the circle becomes a halo: the link between the visual *auréole* and the totally abstract *temps* is difficult to rationalise on its own, though it develops in a more sharply focussed way the idea of circular movement in time as well as space that is suggested by *Un rond de danse*. As so often in modern French poetry, the preposition *de* expresses an extremely imprecise link between nouns: we are simply invited to consider the two ideas simultaneously without seeking to clarify the relationship between them. (English often achieves a similar effect through the use of hyphenated compounds). The next image, adding further detail to the ideas of emotional security and peace that is latent in *cœur* and *douceur*, leads in to the second statement of the stanza, which expresses the complex inter-relationship between the lives of the two participants in the poem, of which the eyes are the vehicle and the symbol. The experience of the two are fused to the extent that the poet's memory of his past life is conditioned not by his awareness of her eyes, but *their* perception of *him*: only what she has seen of him is important.

In demonstrating the effect of the eyes on the poet as an individual, rather than attempting to describe in an objective way a power that may be exerted over others, Eluard's opening stanza is totally different in conception from Porchères's, but the similarity of the theme is nonetheless evident.

In the second stanza direct statement gives way to an accumulation of images, building up a composite structure in which each image is superimposed on the one before without excluding it, in contrast with Porchères's cardhouse structure, which is never allowed to become more than one storey high until the last line of the poem. In contrast to the explicit syntax of Porchères, the syntactic function of Eluard's images is uncertain at the start, and the expectation of a clarification at the end of the sentence remains unfulfilled as far as strict grammar is concerned. A sequence of noun-centred phrases such as these would normally stand in apposition to the subject of a verb which is to follow (in other words they would be prefixed to the word which naturally comes first in the sentence); but in this case Eluard goes further than simply delaying the completion of the sentence, for the subject of the verb that follows (*dépend* in line 14) is not a plural noun to which they could logically be in apposition. There is in fact a break in the syntax (anacoluthon); the images of lines 6-12 are not linked grammatically to what follows. The connection that is not made explicit in the grammar has to be made through imagination; and as we have already seen, imaginative links tend to be more uncertain and ambiguous than grammatical ones. On the one hand we are tempted to associate the images with the singular *Le monde*, despite the grammatical inconsistency – it is after all the subject of the sentence which the sequence of images introduces; but at the same time we tend to make a connection between the images and the only available plural noun, the *yeux* of *de tes yeux purs*, and so link the conclusion of the poem to the dominant theme of the first stanza. However, neither of these interpretations is intrinsically more plausible than the other; the break with the conventional syntax generates an ambiguity that is an integral and essential part of the poem.

The images themselves continue the pattern established in the first stanza, deliberately involving an imprecise connection between ideas which we do not normally associate. They are grouped in an ordered pattern, harmonising with the structure of the stanza and its decasyllabic verses. Lines 6, 7 and 10 consist of expressions formed of two nouns (or noun + adjective in the case of *sourires parfumés*). Lines 8 and 9 are more complex, with the participles *couvrant* and *chargés* introducing a more precise relationship between the two nouns concerned. Lines 11 and 12 complete the series with a yet more complex picture, in which further two-term expressions (*une couvée d'aurores, la paille des astres*) are constituent parts.

Images of this type cannot be *analysed* in the normal sense of the word; all the reader can do is note the associations that the images have for him as an individual. In so doing he may be in part repeating, in part continuing the imaginative processes which gave rise to the poem; he will be filling in for himself the *grandes marges blanches* that Eluard considered to be an essential element in poetry. The principal difference between these images and those used by Porchères is that they do not conform to the traditional definition of a metaphor as a transference of terms based on resemblance; they express the poet's emotional and imaginative response, not a sensory or intellectual perception. Explanations of the kind which Porchères gives for each of his metaphors would be quite impossible in Eluard's poem.

To me *feuilles* suggests both the green vigour of natural growth and the brown falling leaves of autumn; *de jour* adds an idea of light or brightness, but it is an ambiguous idea, for *jour* can be either the light or the duration of day, and there is nothing in the context to emphasise one aspect at the expense of the other. The preposition *de* may mean *composed of*: perhaps light itself comes in leaves, like the leaves of a book. Or *de jour* could mean *by day*: perhaps the *feuilles* are transformed by night. None of these 'interpretations' is right on its own, and indeed the very act of attempting to 'explain' such an image may seem destructive; but they give some idea of the kind of 'liberation' from traditional habits of thought that may be achieved by an original combination of words. The almost unlimited ambiguities of *feuilles de jour* are checked by *mousse de rosée*, where the possible relationship between the two nouns is more restricted. Here perhaps the central idea is of something light, delicate, ephemeral – the foam of a *vin mousseux* perhaps, and the cool, sparkling dew which evaporates in the morning sun – the idea of *jour* remains in our minds behind the next image. The original meaning of *mousse* is *moss*: so in the background there may be a vision of green moss moist with dew. From *rosée* we move on to *roseaux*: associations of words (even arbitrary associations such as this, where there is no common root beneath the phonetically identical syllable) are as natural a part of the imaginative process as associations of *ideas,* though our *conscious* minds tend to reject them as 'irrational' (as indeed they are). The link between *roseaux* and *vent*, on the other hand, is traditional, going back to the biblical *reed shaken with the wind*, and in French particularly to La Fontaine's fable *Le Chêne et le Roseau* and to Lamartine's *le vent qui gémit, le roseau qui soupire* (*Le Lac*, poem no. 25 in this collection). But we would not normally think of saying *roseaux du vent*, nor of using that expression as a metaphor for eyes: imagination is a re-arrangement of existing *données*, coming from actual or aesthetic experience. The principal ideas suggested here are those of fragility, flexibility and movement. With *sourires*, the poem returns briefly to the explicitly human sphere – for smiling eyes involve no great imaginative leap – but the adjective *parfumés* immediately introduces an unexpected element, the presentation of the image in terms of the sense of smell rather than the visual sense with which we normally perceive a smile.

The more extended image of line 8 is perhaps easier to appreciate than the more cryptic images with which the stanza opens, in that the verbal concept, *couvrant*, gives us the key to a picture which we can actually visualise, even though it still involves that imaginative conjunction of things we do not normally envisage together. Here the underlying impression is of a protective, beneficial influence, all-embracing and life-giving. In the following line, however, the two apparent complements of *chargés*, *du ciel et de la mer*, are more obviously at variance with our expectations after *bateaux chargés de*, so we are led to wonder whether they are simply *bateaux du ciel et de la mer* which happen to be *chargés*. Following closely on *le monde*, the elements of sky and sea give an impression of the expanse of the universe, which the eyes nevertheless affect in its totality. The stanza ends with a line that reverts to the original pattern, but is even more neatly symmetrical in that the two images form an antithesis – the eyes which drive away noise are also the bringers of colour.

The atmosphere of sensuous peace and radiance is carried forward into the opening of the final stanza with its complex pattern of inter-related images. The focus of this pattern is the participle *éclos: éclore* originally denotes the hatching of an egg, but in literary French the metaphorical sense of the opening of a flower or the birth of an emotion is predominant. The *couvée des aurores* reminds us of the original sense of *éclos*, enhancing its value as an image for a creative, life-giving force, a refinement and extension of the relatively commonplace *source des couleurs*. Again we have a fusion of senses within a single image: the *parfums* are described in purely visual terms. The following line continues the blend of astronomical imagery with images from the physical reality of everyday life, though shifts in tone are introduced by the fact that *gît sur la paille* evokes the expression *être sur la paille*, meaning to be in poverty, and by the fact that *astres* suggests a more distant and rarified light than *aurores* – the dawns that bring life to the world.

At this point the build-up of images breaks off, and the poem concludes, as it began, with a statement. As we noted earlier, the grammatical and logical function of the images is uncertain, but their poetic function now becomes clear: they provide an imaginative background which enhances and enriches the simple statements of lines 14 and 15. The transition from images to statement is preceded by a formal simile, which prepares for the crucial statement in its structure and in its theme, that of dependence. The parallelism of structure also suggests the possibility that the four terms which compose lines 13-14 might be read diagonally as well as horizontally: all four terms are inter-related through the pivotal word *dépend*. These four terms serve as a kind of résumé of the images of the central portion of the poem, presenting in direct and explicit terms ideas previously conveyed obliquely and imprecisely; the ideas of daylight, innocence, totality and purity are all present in stanza 2. There is, then, a superficial parallel with Porchères in the summary of the images at the end of the poem; but whereas Porchères had left us in no doubt that his images, which are kept vigorously separate throughout the poem, are mutually exclusive, Eluard combines his images to form a single organic whole. Line 14 is the climax of the poem, expressing the idea that love acts as a kind of catalyst that heightens the poet's perception of the world – an idea that is central to much of Eluard's love poetry. However, instead of ending with a rhetorical flourish, as Porchères had done, making it quite clear that there is no more to be said, Eluard extends his conclusion with a further idea, qualifying the apparent simplicity and finality of line 14. Not only do the eyes give meaning to the world, but the poet himself is absorbed into them, and this idea of intercommunicating personalities is expressed in concrete terms through the image of *mon sang coule*. This final line serves to enlarge on the theme of the poem, without actually embarking on a fresh one, so that the poem is 'complete' without being 'finished' as an experience for the reader.

The general similarities in theme and structure between these two poems may now be seen in conjunction with significant differences in outlook, which are only to be expected in poets so widely separated in time. Porchères shows on the one hand a self-conscious mastery of poetic technique in the way in which he juggles with his chosen set of images, and on the other a profound uncertainty as to the nature of things which is if anything reinforced by the vigour of his argument. Both features are aspects of an outlook that many literary historians may label 'Mannerist', seeing it as the literary counterpart of the Mannerist painting and sculpture of the same period.

In Eluard, it is not intellectual rigour that predominates, but the imagination; not a conscious manipulation of ideas, but a deliberate attempt to give scope to the subconscious creation of images. Eluard's natural poetic instincts drew him to play an important part in the Surrealist movement, with its emphasis on the central role of the imagination, released from rational control in all artistic creation. But although written at a time when the Surrealist movement, and Eluard's involvement with it, was at its most vigorous, *La courbe de tes yeux* is not a purely Surrealist poem: the attitude to human experience that it expresses, emphasising the way in which the outside world is transformed through the individual imagination, is certainly Surrealist, but its form and structure set it within the mainstream of the French poetic tradition; it shows little of the iconoclastic defiance characteristic of the theoreticians of the Surrealist movement.

S.A.W.

Marc-Antoine Girard de Saint-Amant, 1594-1661

Le Printemps des environs de Paris

Zéphyr a bien raison d'être amoureux de Flore;
C'est le plus bel objet dont il puisse jouir;
On voit à son éclat les soins s'évanouir
4   Comme les libertés devant l'œil que j'adore.

Qui ne serait ravi d'entendre sous l'aurore
Les miracles volants qu'au bois je viens d'ouïr?
J'en sens avec les fleurs mon cœur s'épanouir,
8   Et mon luth négligé leur veut répondre encore.

L'herbe sourit à l'air d'un air voluptueux;
J'aperçois de ce bord fertile et tortueux
Le doux feu du soleil flatter le sein de l'onde.

12   Le soir et le matin la nuit baise le jour;
Tout aime, tout s'embrase, et je crois que le monde
Ne renaît au printemps que pour mourir d'amour.

(Œuvres, 3ème partie)

Possible comparisons: 13, 27, 38, 42, 76, 79

René Char, 1907-1988

Le Thor

    Dans le sentier aux herbes engourdies où nous nous
étonnions, enfants, que la nuit se risquât à passer,
les guêpes n'allaient plus aux ronces et les oiseaux
aux branches. L'air ouvrait aux hôtes de la matinée sa
5   turbulente immensité. Ce n'étaient que filaments d'ailes,
tentation de crier, voltige entre lumière et transparence.
Le Thor s'exaltait sur la lyre de ses pierres. Le mont
Ventoux, miroir des aigles, était en vue.
    Dans le sentier aux herbes engourdies, la chimère
10   d'un âge perdu souriait à nos jeunes larmes.

(Fureur et Mystère)

© Editions Gallimard

Possible comparisons: 21, 38, 45, 69

These two poems, with three centuries between their respective dates of publication (1649 and 1962), are nevertheless strikingly similar in theme and content. The traditional, almost hackneyed subject of joy at the rebirth of spring, familiar in many national poetic heritages besides our own, is given a perennial, almost archetypal freshness by two poets writing in a very similar vein, but adopting the different poetic conventions and practices of their respective periods. Saint-Amant, the baroque poet representative of the long-neglected pre-classical period of the seventeenth century, but now widely appreciated in the wake of Romanticism for the delicacy and enthusiasm of his natural descriptions; and René Char, a reputedly 'difficult' modern poet who, after his early involvement with Surrealism, discovered a new humanism as a *maquis* leader in the very beautiful terrain of Haute Provence. In order to treat a very similar subject, the one adopts the conventional sonnet form and many of the mythological trappings typical of his time, the other rejects the 'outdated' verse form in favour of the concentrated, self-consciously 'modern' language of the prose poem, but at the same time employs many of the same devices and effects as his predecessor.

Both poems celebrate the beauty of the renewal of nature, and the exhilaration and joy of the poet who experiences it. René Char's poem is perhaps set slightly later in the season – the weather seems warmer, since the *herbes* are *engourdies*, and despite the *turbulente immensité*, *Zéphyr* is a little less in evidence on the banks of the Thor than in the Ile-de-France which provides the décor for Saint-Amant's poem. The regional nature of the setting is emphasised in René Char's idyllic Haute Provence. The little river Thor is personified so as to lose itself in lyrical outpouring, under the watchful eye of the *mont Ventoux*, the well-known landmark of the region. The *environs de Paris*, however, are peopled with mythical gods and goddesses of nature who are by no means limited to the Ile-de-France, and the almost personified birds, flowers, sunshine, water, night and day could equally well be celebrating the coming of spring in any other corner of France. The eagles, wasps and the indeterminate insect presence of *filaments d'ailes* on the other hand suggest the more specific, wilder and perhaps more Mediterranean environment that is typical of René Char's spiritual home and which features in many of his poems.

At the deeper level of the attitude to nature implied by the two poems, there seems to be a great similarity. Both poets are pagan and sensual: very little trace of the Christian mysticism that colours so much Romantic nature poetry. The all-powerful Creator is conspicuous by his absence, and it is the beauty of Creation itself which is being celebrated here. On the other hand the personification which is applied to the elements of both natural décors – *la nuit, l'air, l'herbe* in both poems – makes them larger than life, endows them with a semi-divine spirit on a level with *Zephyr* and *Flore* in the earlier poem. Nature is peopled with independent, almost super-natural forces rivalling each other in expressions of joy and exuberance. In both poems the poet identifies himself as one of these spirits, and attributes his own lyrical function to one of his peers in nature: the birds, *miracles volants* in the second stanza, inspire Saint-Amant to pick up his lute and reply in concert, and René Char follows the example of the singing river Thor and appropriately gives its name to the resulting poem. The life-force that manifests itself in nature is the same as the one which reveals itself in poetry. The emphasis is on the act of creation, not destruction – the only hints of the negative side of nature are neutralised, rendered harmless: *mourir d'amour* for Saint-Amant, the furtive, frightened *nuit*, threatened with absorption by the light in the opening sentence of *Le Thor*. In both poems, the underlying metaphor for the pure living beauty of nature in springtime is of course the Garden of Eden.

Both poets show an innocent and spontaneous enjoyment of the spectacle of nature's bounty, and in both of them it inspires a nostalgia, a memory implied by the way they view the scene, a kind of personal Eden. For Saint-Amant it is the *œil que j'adore* of the first stanza, the imprisoning eye of his mistress, which makes him carefree enough to enjoy the scene, but limits his imaginative freedom so much that he sees everything in terms of love. All the forces of nature are making love to each other, the sexual metaphor is applied to everything, and the world in springtime is lost in passionate embrace. In this respect Saint-Amant is a typical baroque poet, interpreting the world from an intensely personal point of view, inseparable from his emotions. It is tempting to see the René Char poem as inspired by love as well, to make the *nous* into a child-like pair of lovers, but nothing in the text confirms this. What it does show is that the dominant theme of René Char's Eden is that of innocence and wonder. The playful child-like fantasy of the threatened *nuit* in the first sentence leads on to a vision of nature not in love, but at play. The morning air is exuberantly turbulent, and its insect guests are frolicking in a gratuitous expense of movement and energy. The temptation to shout is echoed by the babble of the Thor on its stones. The *chimère d'un âge perdu* is probably a nostalgia for the freshness of vision in childhood, and beyond that a primeval state of innocence when human beings could play carefree in harmony with nature. This second level is not only a dream, but also a delusion, like the Garden of Eden itself.

Whatever the origin of the feelings may be, both poems express states of intense emotion and heightened sensitivity. This is suggested by the theme of lyricism of nature mentioned earlier, and by the use of emotional language to describe the scene: *jouir* and *ravi*, for instance for Saint-Amant and *crier, s'exaltait, larmes* for René Char. Both poems feature a constant use of hyperbole: *le plus bel objet, Tout aime, tout s'embrase* . . . or else *nous nous étonnions, ce n'étaient que . . . voltige entre lumière et transparence*. More interesting is the way both poets use a similar striking poetic conceit to describe the creatures that symbolise the mood of each poem: the birds for Saint-Amant and the insects for René Char. The extreme of poetic excess in *Le Printemps* . . . is the attribution of the concrete adjective *volants* to the abstract noun *miracles*, in the second stanza, whilst the implied *oiseaux* is omitted. This conveys the admiration of the poet at their irrepressible song and the almost invisible movement. A very similar effect is created by the metonymy of *filaments d'ailes* referring to the unmentioned insects whose wing movements alone can be glimpsed during their *voltige entre lumière et transparence*: they move so quickly that they are hardly distinguishable and seem transparent against the light which seems all the more dazzling. In both these examples a strongly emotional response to a vivid perception is rendered by an extreme poetic effect.

The two poems also share a deeper level of thematic suggestiveness which perhaps accounts for the intensity of emotional response that they express. Both contain hints of a level of quasi-allegory at which moral issues are touched upon. Already the underlying metaphor of the Garden of Eden brings with it a group of moral preoccupations. The nostalgia for the Garden of Eden implies a desire to escape from civilisation, to get away from the corruption of man in society, which does seem to be reflected in the two poems. If nature seems so beautiful it is by contrast with civilisation, and if love and childhood are so attractive it is as an escape from the constraints and responsibilities of adult society. For Saint-Amant, the beauty of the flora or the beauty of his mistress make all cares vanish away; but paradoxically this new found freedom brings a new constraint, that of faithfulness to his mistress whose eye denies his *libertés*. Even in an idyllic Garden of Eden he cannot share the freedom of the winds, the birds and the flowers. For René Char, the banks of the Thor represent an escape into a world of childhood spontaneity and innocence, an aspiration towards lucidity and freedom which are perhaps symbolised by light and movement in this poem, as they often are in other poems of the same collection. But the myth of the freedom of the Garden of Eden is an illusion, a *chimère* like the *miroir des alouettes* used to attract and trap birds. But the birds are not larks, but eagles hovering over the clearly visible *mont Ventoux,* perhaps symbolising the mobility and controlled equilibrium of the poet himself and the clarity of his visions and aspirations. The idyllic garden of the banks of the Thor represents an attractive ideal, but an illusory one that must be transcended, even at the cost of our innocence and our tears.

For all the similarity of themes and poetic effects which extends even to the imaginative hinterland of the two poems, they remain strongly in contrast at the level of their form. Saint-Amant adopts a conventional alexandrine sonnet form to deal with a conventional subject, spring, and he later inserted the sonnet into a series on the four seasons. He also makes considerable use of current mythology to represent the wind and the flowers, and uses the common device of personification throughout the poem. The effect of this is in accordance with the original intention, which he shares with many of his contemporaries: the theme is given a general, universal relevance which nonetheless borders on the banal. Yet as we have seen these features are set against a number of very personal poetic effects and an extremely subjective vision which contrast with the formal conventionality, and give the poem a more interesting and complex resonance. It is as if the conflict between emotional freedom and formal constraint were present also at the level of the form of the poem. The form of the poem is also noticeable for a subtle musicality produced by the use of resonant rhyming vowels (-ore, -ouir, -eux, -onde, -our) and a discreet alliteration (*Le doux feu du Soleil flatter le sein de l'Onde*). This helps to emphasise the lyrical and emotional treatment of the subject, whilst the rhymes, mostly rich, maintain a strong formal structure.

René Char, on the other hand, deliberately avoids all the trappings of conventional poetic form by writing in prose. Yet many features of the text indicate to the reader that he is reading a poem and create an alternative poetic structure, which is a common characteristic of prose poetry. The brevity and the typographical space around the text already suggest a short, dense, epigrammatic poem. The complex syntax of the first sentence, with the word *enfants* unusually set in apposition in a subordinate clause, suggests the poetic intention of the style. The personification of *la nuit, l'air* and *le Thor* give the text a symbolic resonance, and the parataxis of *filaments d'ailes, tentation de crier, voltige entre lumière et transparence* creates a complex image and a rhythmic pattern. The short second, fourth and fifth sentences each describe a feature of the landscape and set up a pattern within the first paragraph. The repetition of *Dans le sentier aux herbes engourdies* in the last sentence-paragraph gives a sense of conclusion to the text, rounding it off in a poetic way. In fact the tension between lyrical freedom and formal structure exists in this poem too, but with a difference of emphasis: it could almost be described as a sonnet in prose.

There is a further formal level at which the two poems are in contrast with each other. Saint-Amant writes in the first person singular and in the present tense in this poem, giving it an immediacy and directness which suggests that the poet is witnessing the scene as he writes. It also emphasises the personal, subjective and spontaneous nature of the sentiments he expresses. René Char on the other hand, writes in the first person plural and uses the imperfect tense. This has the effect of blurring the presence of the author in the poem in favour of a *we* that is not clearly defined: is he speaking royally, for himself, for a couple, for his friends, or for the whole of mankind? Probably for a childhood companion, but the other possibilities are not excluded, and broaden the implications of the poem. The imperfect gives the tone of nostalgia mentioned earlier, and a sense of rooted familiarity with what is described: we know that it represents an important experience from the poet's past.

The points of comparison between the two poems are so numerous, and even extend far into their imaginative resonance, that it is tempting to see them as two re-workings of a myth as old as the French poetic tradition itself. They can be seen as two variations on the perennial theme of the innocence and freshness of the rebirth of the natural cycle in Spring, both coloured by the poetic conventions of their time, but nonetheless employing essentially the same range of associations and rhetorical devices. This observation provides good evidence for the way in which poetic tradition is self-referential, with the rhetorical structures referring back consciously or otherwise to aspects of the tradition by which they were established; and the themes drawing on a reservoir of mythical subjects constantly re-invented by each new generation of poets. Despite the similarities, both poems are typical and representative of their authors; but neither expresses a major insight central to the author's work. They are both successful, but not distinctive poems and each provides an example typical of poetry not only of the author, but also of the period in which it was written.

P.G.H.

Suggestions for further reading

The following works extend or complement in various ways the approach adopted in this volume:

A. On the technique of commentary:

Howarth, W. D. and Walton, C. L.: *Explications: The Technique of French Literary Appreciation* (Oxford, 1971)
>A thorough introduction to the theory and practice of *explication,* followed by examples from different periods and genres.

Nurse, P. H. (ed.): *The Art of Criticism: Essays in French Literary Analysis* (Edinburgh, 1969)
>An anthology of commentaries by different critics, experts on the authors concerned; it illustrates the diversity of approach that may stem from the critic's priorities as well as from the passages under discussion.

B. On poetic language:

Nowottny, Winifred: *The Language Poets Use* (London, 1962)
>Predominantly concerned with English poetry, but raising questions which, for the most part, are equally relevant to French. A thought-provoking book.

C. On versification:

Delbouille, P.: *La sonorité des vers* (Paris, 1961)
>An extended but very well balanced treatment of a difficult but important aspect.

Grammont, M.: *Petit Traité de versification française* (Paris, 1908, and many subsequent reprints)
>A peremptory but useful summary of the sometimes controversial views advanced at length in the same author's *Le Vers Français.*

Giraud, P.: *La Versification* (Paris, 1970)
>The best introduction to the subject, a model of lucidity and compressed scholarship.

Scott, Clive: *French Verse Art* (Cambridge, 1980)
>A penetrating study of French versification as an aspect of poetry, not simply a technique.

Suberville, J.: *Histoire et théorie de la versification française* (Paris, n.d.)

    A *manuel scolaire,* admirably clear but dogmatic and normative in approach to twentieth-century developments.

D.   On poetry as *form*:

Joubert, J. -L.: *La Poésie* (Paris, 1977)

    A manageable introduction to recent French thinking on the nature of poetry.

Lewis, Roy: *On reading French verse* (Oxford, 1982)

E.   On terminology:

Fowler, R: *A Dictionary of Modern Critical Terms* (London, 1973)

    A commonsense approach to terminology as a means to an end, not a self-sufficient jargon.

More comprehensive information is available in:

    Preminger, A.: *Encyclopaedia of Poetry and Poetics* (Princeton, 1965), and in

    Morier, H.: *Dictionnaire de poétique et de rhétorique* (Paris, 1975)

It will be noted that the majority of the works listed here are by English-speaking critics, and directed at an English-speaking audience; this is not the result of any prejudice against French critics, but of the awareness that French criticism presupposes a background of French culture, and may therefore pass over matters that can prove major stumbling blocks to foreign readers. We hope that students will increasingly turn to *French* critical works as they find their own critical feet.

1

François Villon, 1431-1463?

Ballade des Dames du Temps Jadis

Dites-moi où, n'en quel pays
Est Flore la belle Romaine,
Archipiades ni Thaïs,
4   Qui fut sa cousine germaine,
Echo, parlant quand bruit on mène
Dessus rivière ou sous étang
Qui beauté eut trop plus qu'humaine.
8   Mais où sont les neiges d'antan?

Où est la très sage Héloïs
Pour qui châtré fut et puis moinc
Pierre Abelard à Saint Denis?
12   Pour son amour eut cette essoine.
Semblablement où est la reine
Qui commanda que Buridan
Fut jeté en un sac en Seine?
16   Mais où sont les neiges d'antan?

La reine Blanche comme lis
Qui chantait à voix de sirène,
Berthe au grand pied, Biétris, Alis,
20   Haremburgis qui tint le Maine,
Et Jehanne la bonne Lorraine
Qu'Anglais brûlèrent à Rouen;
Où sont-ils, où, Vierge souvraine?
24   Mais où sont les neiges d'antan?

Prince, n'enquerez de semaine
Où elles sont, ni de cet an,
Qu'à ce refrain ne vous ramène:
28   "Mais où sont les neiges d'antan?"

(Le Testament)

7	trop plus: beaucoup plus
12	essoine: peine
23	où sont-ils: *ils* for *elles* is permissible in 15th century French
25	enquerez: demandez
27	"Lest this refrain be recalled to you"

Possible comparisons: 20, 80

1

Joachim Du Bellay, 1522-1560

Dialogue d'un Amoureux et d'Echo

Piteuse Echo, qui erres en ces bois
Réponds au son de ma dolente voix.
D'où ai-je pu ce grand mal concevoir,
Qui m'ôte ainsi de raison le devoir?   De voir.
5   Qui est l'auteur de ces maux avenus?   Vénus.
Comment en sont tous mes sens devenus?   Nus.
Qu'étais-je avant d'entrer en ce passage?   Sage.
Et maintenant que sens-je en mon courage?   Rage.
Qu'est-ce qu'aimer, et s'en plaindre souvent?   Vent.
10   Que suis-je donc, lorsque mon cœur en fend?   Enfant.
Qui est la fin de prison si obscure?   Cure.
Dis-moi, quelle est celle pour qui j'endure?   Dure.
Sent-elle bien la douleur qui me point?   Point.
Oh, que cela me vient bien mal à point!
15   Me faut-il donc, (ô débile entreprise)
Lâcher ma proie avant que l'avoir prise?
Si vaut-il mieux avoir cœur moins hautain,
Qu'ainsi languir sous espoir incertain.

(Recueil de Poésie)

Possible comparisons: 8, 41

Joachim Du Bellay, 1522-1560

D'un vanneur de blé aux vents

A vous, troupe légère,
Qui d'aile passagère
Par le monde volez,
Et d'un sifflant murmure
L'ombrageuse verdure
6   Doucement ébranlez,

J'offre ces violettes,
Ces lis et ces fleurettes,
Et ces roses ici,
Ces vermeillettes roses,
Tout fraîchement écloses,
12   Et ces œillets aussi.

De votre douce haleine
Eventez cette plaine,
Eventez ce séjour;
Cependant que j'ahane
A mon blé, que je vanne
18   A la chaleur du jour.

(Divers Jeux Rustiques)

15   séjour: demeure

Possible comparison: 46

Joachim Du Bellay, 1522–1560

Métamorphose d'une Rose

Comme sur l'arbre sec la veuve tourterelle
Regrette ses amours d'une triste querelle,
Ainsi de mon mari le trépas gémissant,
4   En pleurs je consumais mon âge languissant;

Quand pour chasser de moi cette tristesse enclose,
Mon destin consentit que je devinsse Rose,
Qui d'un poignant hallier se hérisse à l'entour,
8   Pour faire résistance aux assauts de l'Amour.

Je suis, comme j'étais, d'odeur naïve et franche,
Mes bras sont transformés en épineuse branche,
Mes pieds en tige verte, et tout le demeurant
12   De mon corps est changé en Rosier bien fleurant.

Les plis de mon habit sont écailleuses pointes,
Qui en rondeur égale autour de moi sont jointes;
Et ce qui entr'ouvert montre un peu de rougeur,
16   Imite de mon ris la première douceur.

Mes cheveux sont changés en feuilles qui verdoient,
Et ces petits rayons, qui vivement flamboient
Au centre de ma Rose, imitent de mes yeux
20   Les feux jadis égaux à deux flammes des cieux.

La beauté de mon teint à l'aurore pareille
N'a du sang de Vénus pris sa couleur vermeille,
Mais de cette rougeur que la pudicité
24   Imprime sur le front de la virginité.

Les grâces, dont le ciel m'avait favorisée,
Or'que Rose je suis, me servent de rosée;
Et l'honneur qui en moi a fleuri si longtemps,
28   S'y garde encore entier d'un éternel printemps.

La plus longue fraîcheur des roses est bornée
Par le cours naturel d'une seule journée;
Mais cette gaieté qu'on voit en moi fleurir,
32   Par l'injure du temps ne pourra dépérir.

A nul je ne défends ni l'odeur ni la vue,
Mais si quelqu'indiscret voulait à l'impourvue
S'en approcher trop près, il ne s'en irait point
36   Sans éprouver comment ma chaste rigueur point.

Que nul n'espère donc de ravir cette Rose,
Puisqu'au jardin d'honneur elle est si bien enclose;
Où plus soigneusement elle est gardée encor
40   Que du Dragon veillant n'étaient les pommes d'or.

Celui que la vertu a choisi pour sa guide,
Ce sera celui seul qui en sera l'Alcide;
A lui seul j'ouvrirai la porte du verger,
44   Où heureux il pourra me cueillir sans danger

(Divers Jeux Rustiques)

2	querelle : plainte, lamentation
7	poignant : épineux
9	naïve : fraîche
12	fleurant : fleurissant
16	ris : sourire
32	injure : flétrissure
40	Dragon : the dragon Ladon, set by Hera as a guard on the tree bearing the Golden Apples of the Sun.
42	Alcide : Hercules, whose eleventh Labour was to steal the Golden Apples.

Possible comparisons :33, 36, 37

Pierre de Ronsard, 1524–1585

'Marie, levez-vous'

Marie, levez-vous, vous êtes paresseuse,
Jà la gaie alouette au ciel a fredonné,
Et jà le rossignol doucement jargonné,
4   Dessus l'épine assis, sa complainte amoureuse.

Sus debout! allons voir l'herbelette perleuse,
Et votre beau rosier de boutons couronné,
Et vos œillets mignons auxquels aviez donné
8   Hier au soir de l'eau d'une main si soigneuse.

Hier soir en vous couchant vous jurâtes vos yeux,
D'être plus tôt que moi ce matin éveillée;
Mais le dormir de l'aube, aux filles gracieux,

12   Vous tient d'un doux sommeil encor les yeux sillée.
Çà! çà! que je les baise, et votre beau tétin
Cent fois pour vous apprendre à vous lever matin.

(Les Amours de Marie)

Possible comparisons: 77, 79

Pierre de Ronsard, 1524–1585

Chanson

Plus étroit que la vigne à l'ormeau se marie
    De bras souplement forts,
Du lien de tes mains, Maîtresse, je te prie,
4   Enlace-moi le corps.

Et feignant de dormir, d'une mignarde face
    Sur mon front penche-toi;
Inspire, en me baisant, ton haleine et ta grâce
8   Et ton cœur dedans moi.

Puis appuyant ton sein sur le mien qui se pâme,
    Pour mon mal apaiser,
Serre plus fort mon col, et me redonne l'âme
12   Par l'esprit d'un baiser.

Si tu me fais ce bien, par tes yeux je te jure,
    Serment qui m'est si cher,
Que de tes bras aimés jamais autre aventure
16   Ne pourra m'arracher.

Mais souffrant doucement le joug de ton empire,
    Tant soit-il rigoureux,
Dans les Champs Elysés une même navire
20   Nous passera tous deux.

Là, morts de trop aimer, sous les branches myrtines,
    Nous verrons tous les jours
Les anciens héros auprès des héroïnes
24   Ne parler que d'amours.

Tantôt nous danserons par les fleurs des rivages
    Sous maints accords divers,
Tantôt, lassés du bal, irons sous les ombrages
28   Des lauriers toujours verts,

Où le mollet Zéphire en haletant secoue
    De soupirs printaniers
Ores les orangers, ores mignard se joue
32   Entre les citronniers.

Là du plaisant avril la saison immortelle
    Sans échange se suit;
La terre sans labeur de sa grasse mamelle
36   Toute chose y produit.

D'en bas la troupe sainte autrefois amoureuse,
    Nous honorant sur tous,
Viendra nous saluer, s'estimant bienheureuse
40   De s'accointer de nous.

Puis nous faisant asseoir dessus l'herbe fleurie,
    De toutes au milieu,
Nulle en se retirant ne sera point marrie
44   De nous quitter son lieu,

Non celle qu'un taureau sous une peau menteuse
    Emporta par la mer,
Non celle qu'Apollon vit, vierge dépiteuse,
48   En laurier se former,

Ni celles qui s'en vont toutes tristes ensemble,
    Artémise et Didon,
Ni cette belle Grecque à qui ta beauté semble
52   Comme tu fais de nom.

(Amours Diverses)

21   myrtines : de myrthe. The myrtle tree is sacred to Venus; it is in a forest of myrtle that Aeneas, in his journey to the underworld in the sixth book of the Aeneid, meets the the ghost of Dido and of other famous lovers.

45   allusion to the myth of Europa.

47   allusion to the myth of Apollo and Daphne.

49   Artémise: Artemisia, widow of the king Mausolus of Caria, was famous in antiquity for her love for her husband and for the tomb (Mausoleum) she caused to be erected in his memory.

51   semble: modern French *ressemble*. The allusion is to Helen of Troy; the poem was first published in the collection entitled *Sonnets pour Hélène* (1578), before reappearing in this slightly modified form in the *Amours Diverses* in 1584.

Possible comparison: 42

7

Agrippa d'Aubigné, 1551-1630

Stances

Liberté douce et gracieuse,
Des petits animaux le plus riche trésor,
Ah! liberté, combien es-tu plus précieuse
Ni que les perles ni que l'or!

4

Suivant par les bois à la chasse
Les écureuils sautants, moi qui étais captif,
Envieux de leur bien, leur malheur je prochasse,
Et en pris un entier et vif.

8

J'en fis présent à ma mignonne
Qui lui tressa de soie un cordon pour prison;
Mais les friands appats du sucre qu'on lui donne
Lui sont plus mortels que poison.

12

Les mains de neige qui le lient,
Les attirants regards qui le vont décevant
Plutôt obstinément à la mort le convient
Qu'être prisonnier et vivant.

16

Las! comment ne suis-je semblable
Au petit écureuil qui, étant arrêté
Meurt de regrets sans fin, et n'a si agréable
Sa vie que la liberté?

20

O douce fin de triste vie
De ce cœur qui choisit la mort pour ses malheurs,
Qui pour le surmonter sacrifie sa vie
Au regret des champs et des fleurs!

24

Ainsi, après mille batailles,
Vengeant leur liberté on a vu les Romains
Planter leurs chauds poignards en leur vives entrailles
Se guérir pour être inhumains.

28

Mais tant s'en faut que je ruine
Ma vie et ma prison, qu'elle me plaît si fort,
Qu'en riant je gazouille, ainsi que fait le cygne,
Les douces chansons de ma mort.

32

(Le Printemps)

7   leur malheur je prochasse : je cherche à leur faire mal

Possible comparisons : 13, 17, 36, 67

8

Jacques Davy, Cardinal du Perron, 1555–1618

'Au bord tristement doux'

Au bord tristement doux des eaux, je me retire,
Et vois couler ensemble et les eaux et mes jours:
Je m'y vois sec et pâle, et si j'aime toujours
4 Leur rêveuse mollesse où ma peine se mire.

Au plus secret des bois je conte mon martyre,
Je pleure mon martyre en chantant mes amours,
Et si j'aime les bois, et les bois les plus sourds,
8 Quand j'ai jeté mes cris, me les viennent redire.

Dame dont les beautés me possèdent si fort,
Qu'étant absent de vous je n'aime que la mort,
Les eaux en votre absence, et les bois me consolent;

12 Je vois dedans les eaux, j'entends dedans les bois,
L'image de mon teint et celle de ma voix,
Toutes peintes de morts, qui nagent et qui volent.

(1598)

3 et si : et pourtant

Possible comparisons : 2, 25, 27, 35

François de Malherbe, 1555–1628

Sonnet

Beaux et grands bâtiments d'éternelle structure,
Superbes de matière, et d'ouvrages divers,
Où le plus digne roi qui soit en l'univers
4   Aux miracles de l'art fait céder la nature,

Beau parc et beaux jardins, qui dans votre clôture
Avez toujours des fleurs et des ombrages verts,
Non sans quelque démon qui défend aux hivers
8   D'en effacer jamais l'agréable peinture,

Lieux qui donnez aux cœurs tant d'aimables désirs,
Bois, fontaines, canaux, si parmi vos plaisirs
Mon humeur est chagrine, et mon visage triste:

12   Ce n'est point qu'en effet vous n'ayez des appas,
Mais quoi que vous ayez, vous n'avez point Caliste,
Et moi je ne vois rien quand je ne la vois pas.

(1609)

Possible comparisons: 11, 13, 15

François de Malherbe, 1555-1628

Paraphrase du Psaume cxlv
Stances

N'espérons plus, mon âme, aux promesses du monde;
Sa lumière est un verre, et sa faveur une onde
Que toujours quelque vent empêche de calmer.
Quittons ces vanités, lassons-nous de les suivre;
    C'est Dieu qui nous fait vivre,
6   C'est Dieu qu'il faut aimer.

En vain, pour satisfaire à nos lâches envies,
Nous passons près des rois tout le temps de nos vies
A souffrir des mépris et ployer les genoux:
Ce qu'ils peuvent n'est rien; ils sont, comme nous sommes,
    Véritablement hommes,
12   Et meurent comme nous.

Ont-ils rendu l'esprit, ce n'est plus que poussière
Que cette majesté si pompeuse et si fière,
Dont l'éclat orgueilleux étonnait l'univers;
Et, dans ces grands tombeaux où leurs âmes hautaines
    Font encore les vaines,
18   Ils sont mangés des vers.

Là se perdent ces noms de maîtres de la terre,
D'arbitres de la paix, de foudres de la guerre;
Comme ils n'ont plus de sceptre, ils n'ont plus de flatteurs;
Et tombent avec eux d'une chute commune
    Tous ceux que leur fortune
24   Faisait leurs serviteurs.

(1627)

Title : Psalm 145 according to the Vulgate (and Greek Septuagint) = Psalm 146 in the Authorised Version. The paraphrase omits the first two and last two verses.

Possible comparisons : 15, 27, 31, 42

Théophile de Viau, 1590-1626

A Monsieur Du Fargis

Je ne m'y puis résoudre, excuse-moi, de grâce:
Ecrivant pour autrui je me sens tout de glace;
Je te promis chez toi des vers pour un amant
Qui se veut faire aider à plaindre son tourment,
5 Mais pour lui satisfaire, et bien peindre sa flamme,
Je voudrais par avant avoir connu son âme.
Tu sais bien que chacun a des goûts tout divers,
Qu'il faut à chaque esprit une sorte de vers,
Et que pour bien ranger le discours et l'étude,
10 En matière d'amour je suis un peu trop rude;
Il faudrait comme Ovide avoir été piqué:
On écrit aisément ce qu'on a pratiqué.
Et je te jure ici, sans faire le farouche,
Que de ce feu d'amour aucun trait ne me touche;
15 Je n'entends point les lois ni les façons d'aimer,
Ni comment Cupidon se mêle de charmer:
Cette divinité des dieux même adorée,
Ces traits d'or et de plomb, cette trousse dorée,
Ces ailes, ces brandons, ces carquois, ces appas,
20 Sont vraiment un mystère où je ne pense pas.
La sotte antiquité nous a laissé des fables
Qu'un homme de bon sens ne croit point recevables,
Et jamais son esprit ne trouvera bien sain
Celui-là qui se paît d'un fantôme si vain,
25 Qui se laisse emporter à des confus mensonges,
Et vient même en veillant s'embarrasser de songes.
Le vulgaire, qui n'est qu'erreur, qu'illusion,
Trouve du sens caché dans la confusion,
Même des plus savants, mais non pas des plus sages
30 Expliquent aujourd'hui ces fabuleux ombrages.
Autrefois les mortels parlaient avec les dieux;
On en voyait pleuvoir à toute heure des cieux;
Quelquefois on a vu prophétiser des bêtes;
Les arbres de Dodone étaient aussi prophètes.
35 Ces contes sont fâcheux à des esprits hardis,
Qui sentent autrement qu'on ne faisait jadis.
Sur ce propos un jour j'espère de t'écrire,
Et prendre un doux loisir pour nous donner à rire;
Cependant je te prie encore m'excuser,
40 Et me laisser ainsi libre à te refuser,

Me permettre toujours de te fermer l'oreille
Quand tu me prieras d'une faveur pareille.
Penses-tu, quand j'aurais employé tout un jour
A bien imaginer des passions d'amour,
45   Que mes conceptions seraient bien exprimées
En paroles de choix, bien mises, bien rimées?
L'autre n'y trouverait, possible, rien pour lui,
Tant il est malaisé d'écrire pour autrui.
Après qu'à son plaisir j'aurais donné ma peine,
50   Je sais bien que possible il louerait ma veine:
"Vraiment ces vers sont beaux, ils sont doux et coulants,
Mais pour ma passion ils sont un peu trop lents;
J'eusse bien désiré que vous eussiez encore
Mieux loué sa beauté, car vraiment je l'honore;
55   Vous n'avez point parlé du front, ni des cheveux,
Ni de son bel esprit, seul objet de mes vœux.
Tant seulement six vers encor je vous supplie
Mon Dieu! que de travail vous donne ma folie!"
Il voudrait que son front fût aux astres pareils,
60   Que je la fisse ensemble et l'aube et le soleil;
Que j'écrive comment ses regards sont des armes,
Comme il verse pour elle un océan de larmes.
Ces termes égarés offensent mon humeur,
Et ne viennent qu'au sens d'un novice rimeur,
65   Qui réclame Phœbus; quant à moi, je l'abjure,
Et ne reconnais rien pour tout que ma nature.

(Œuvres, première partie)

11   reference to Ovid's *Ars Amatoria* (The Art of Love)

18   Cupid's gold-tipped arrows brought happy love, the leaden ones suffering.

20   où : à quoi

33   an Old Testament reference : Balaam's ass in the Book of Numbers (chapter 20)

34   The oak trees at Dodona, sacred to Zeus, gave oracles through the rustling of their leaves.

47   possible : peut-être

65   réclame : 'call upon', 'invoke'. Phœbus was the God of poetic inspiration; in the early seventeenth century, *parler Phœbus* was a derogatory term applied to writers who used an elaborate and artificial style.

Possible comparisons : 9, 13, 23, 75

Théophile de Viau, 1590–1626

Sonnet

Ton orgueil peut durer au plus deux ou trois ans;
Après cette beauté ne sera plus si vive;
Tu verras que ta flamme alors sera tardive,
4   Et que tu deviendras l'objet des médisants.

Tu seras le refus de tous les courtisans;
Les plus sots laisseront ta passion oisive,
Et tes désirs honteux d'une amitié lascive
8   Tenteront un valet à force de présents.

Tu chercheras à qui te donner pour maîtresse;
On craindra ton abord, on fuira ta caresse;
Un chacun de partout te donnera congé;

12   Tu reviendras à moi, je n'en ferai nul compte,
Tu pleureras d'amour, je rirai de ta honte:
Lors tu seras punie, et je serai vengé.

(*Œuvres,* première partie)

Possible comparisons: 13, 14, 20

Vincent Voiture, 1598–1648

'La terre brillante de fleurs'

La terre brillante de fleurs
Fait éclater mille couleurs,
D'aujourd'hui seulement connues;
L'astre du jour, en souriant,
Jette sur la face des nues
6   L'or et l'azur dont il peint l'orient.

Le ciel est couvert de saphirs,
Les doux et gracieux zéphyrs
Soupirent mieux que de coutume;
L'aurore a le teint plus vermeil,
Et semble que le jour s'allume
12   D'un plus beau feu que celui du soleil.

Les oiseaux aux charmantes voix,
Mieux que jamais dedans ces bois,
Se font une amoureuse guerre;
Sans doute la troupe des dieux
A quitté le ciel pour la terre,
18   Ou la divine Oronte est en ces lieux.

Oronte dont les yeux vainqueurs
Ont assujetti mille cœurs,
Dont elle refuse l'hommage;
Qui naissant a reçu des cieux
Toutes les grâces en partage,
24   Et les faveurs des hommes et des dieux.

Par la force de ses attraits
Ces vieux troncs, ces noires forêts,
Ressentent l'amoureuse flamme;
Tout cède à des charmes si chers,
Et ses yeux qui nous ôtent l'âme,
30   D'un seul regard la donnent aux rochers.

Ainsi sortant de Fontenay,
Dedans le chemin de Gournay,
Faisant des vers à l'aventure,
Suivant l'humeur qui l'emportait,
L'insensible et le froid Voiture
36   Parlait d'amour comme s'il en sentait.

Les nymphes des eaux et des bois,
Ecoutant sa dolente voix,
Ne purent s'empêcher de rire;
Mais un faune qui l'entendit,
Aux dryades se prit à dire,
42   Possible est-il plus vrai qu'il ne le dit.

(1650)

42   Possible: peut-être

Possible comparisons: VIa, 7, 11, 20, 38, 52, 76

Pierre Corneille, 1606-1684

Stances à Marquise

Marquise, si mon visage
A quelques traits un peu vieux,
Souvenez-vous qu'à mon âge
4   Vous ne vaudrez guère mieux.

Le temps aux plus belles choses
Se plaît à faire un affront,
Et saura faner vos roses
8   Comme il a ridé mon front.

Le même cours des planètes
Règle nos jours et nos nuits,
On m'a vu ce que vous êtes;
12   Vous serez ce que je suis.

Cependant j'ai quelques charmes
Qui sont assez éclatants
Pour n'avoir trop d'alarmes
16   De ces ravages du temps.

Vous en avez qu'on adore,
Mais ceux que vous méprisez
Pourraient bien durer encore
20   Quand ceux-là seront usés.

Ils pourront sauver la gloire
Des yeux qui me semblent doux,
Et dans mille ans faire croire
24   Ce qu'il me plaira de vous.

Chez cette race nouvelle
Où j'aurai quelque crédit,
Vous ne passerez pour belle
28   Qu'autant que je l'aurai dit.

Pensez-y, belle Marquise:
Quoiqu'un grison fasse effroi,
Il vaut bien qu'on le courtise,
32   Quand il est fait comme moi.

(1660)

Possible comparisons: 20, 40, 80

Paul Scarron, 1610–1660

'Superbes monuments'

Superbes monuments de l'orgueil des humains,
Pyramides, tombeaux, dont la vaine structure
A témoigné que l'art, par l'adresse des mains
4   Et l'assidu travail, peut vaincre la nature;

Vieux palais ruinés, chefs-d'œuvre des Romains
Et le dernier effort de leur architecture,
Colisée où souvent les peuples inhumains
8   De s'entr'assassiner se donnaient tablature;

Par l'injure du temps vous êtes abolis
Ou, du moins, la plupart, on vous a démolis:
Il n'est point de ciment que le temps ne dissoude.

12   Si vos marbres si durs ont senti son pouvoir,
Dois-je trouver mauvais qu'un méchant pourpoint noir
Qui m'a duré deux ans soit troué par le coude?

(1651)

Possible comparisons : 9, 10, 45, 51, 76, 80

Paul Scarron, 1610–1660

Sonnet sur Paris

Un amas confus de maisons,
Des crottes dans toutes les rues,
Ponts, églises, palais, prisons,
4   Boutiques bien ou mal pourvues;

Force gens noirs, blancs, roux, grisons,
Des prudes, des filles perdues,
Des meurtres et des trahisons,
8   Des gens de plume aux mains crochues;

Maint poudré qui n'a point d'argent,
Maint homme qui craint le sergent,
Maint fanfaron qui toujours tremble,

12   Pages, lacquais, voleurs de nuit,
Carrosses, chevaux, et grand bruit,
C'est là Paris. Que vous en semble?

(1654)

Possible comparisons: 49, 51, 73

Charles de Marguetel de Saint Denis
de Saint-Evremond, 1613-1703

'Nature, enseigne-moi'

Nature, enseigne-moi par quel bizarre effort
Notre âme hors de nous est quelquefois ravie;
Dis-nous comme à nos corps elle-même asservie
4   S'agite, s'assoupit, se réveille, s'endort.

Les moindres animaux, plus heureux dans leur sort,
Vivent innocemment sans crainte et sans envie,
Exempts de mille soins qui traversent la vie
8   Et de mille frayeurs que nous donne la mort.

Un mélange incertain d'esprit et de matière
Nous fait vivre avec trop ou trop peu de lumière
Pour savoir justement et nos biens et nos maux.

12   Change l'état douteux dans lequel tu nous ranges;
Nature, élève-nous à la clarté des anges,
Ou nous abaisse au sens des simples animaux!

Possible comparisons: 7, 18, 26, 76

Jean de La Fontaine, 1621-1695

Le Lièvre et les Grenouilles

Un lièvre en son gîte songeait
(Car que faire en un gîte, à moins que l'on ne songe?);
Dans un profond ennui ce lièvre se plongeait:
Cet animal est triste, et la crainte le ronge.
5   Les gens de naturel peureux
        Sont, disait-il, bien malheureux;
Ils ne sauraient manger morceau qui leur profite.
Jamais un plaisir pur, toujours assauts divers:
Voilà comme je vis: cette crainte maudite
10   M'empêche de dormir, sinon les yeux ouverts.
Corrigez-vous, dira quelque sage cervelle.
        Et la peur se corrige-t-elle?
        Je crois même qu'en bonne foi
        Les hommes ont peur comme moi.
15   Ainsi raisonnait notre lièvre
        Et cependant faisait le guet.
        Il était douteux, inquiet:
Un souffle, une ombre, un rien, tout lui donnait la fièvre.
        Le mélancolique animal,
20   En rêvant à cette matière,
Entend un léger bruit: ce lui fut un signal
        Pour s'enfuir devers sa tanière.
Il s'en alla passer sur le bord d'un étang.
Grenouilles aussitôt de sauter dans les ondes,
25   Grenouilles de rentrer dans leurs grottes profondes.
        Oh! dit-il, j'en fais faire autant
        Qu'on m'en fait faire! Ma présence
Effraie aussi les gens, je mets l'alarme au camp!
        Et d'où me vient cette vaillance?
30   Comment! des animaux qui tremblent devant moi!
        Je suis donc un foudre de guerre?
Il n'est, je le vois bien, si poltron sur la terre
Qui ne puisse trouver un plus poltron que soi.

(Fables)

Possible comparisons : 7, 17, 24, 63, 68, 70

19

Jean de La Fontaine, 1621-1695

Le Renard, le Loup et le Cheval

Un renard, jeune encor, quoique des plus madrés,
Vit le premier cheval qu'il eût vu de sa vie.
Il dit à certain loup, franc novice: Accourez:
 Un animal paît dans nos prés,
5 Beau, grand; j'en ai la vue encor toute ravie.
– Est-il plus fort que nous? dit le loup en riant.
 Fais-moi son portrait, je te prie.
– Si j'étais quelque peintre ou quelque étudiant,
Repartit le renard, j'avancerais la joie
10 Que vous aurez en le voyant.
Mais venez. Que sait-on? peut-être est-ce une proie
 Que la Fortune nous envoie.
Ils vont; et le cheval, qu'à l'herbe on avait mis,
Assez peu curieux de semblables amis,
15 Fut presque sur le point d'enfiler la venelle.
Seigneur, dit le renard, vos humbles serviteurs
Apprendraient volontiers comment on vous appelle.
Le cheval, qui n'était dépourvu de cervelle,
Leur dit: Lisez mon nom, vous le pouvez, Messieurs:
20 Mon cordonnier l'a mis autour de ma semelle.
Le renard s'excusa sur son peu de savoir.
Mes parents, reprit-il, ne m'ont point fait instruire;
Ils sont pauvres et n'ont qu'un trou pour tout avoir.
Ceux du loup, gros messieurs, l'ont fait apprendre à lire.
25 Le loup, par ce discours flatté,
  S'approcha; mais sa vanité
Lui coûta quatre dents: le cheval lui desserre
Un coup; et haut le pied. Voilà mon loup par terre
  Mal en point, sanglant et gâté.
30 Frère, dit le renard, ceci nous justifie
  Ce que m'ont dit des gens d'esprit:
Cet animal vous a sur la mâchoire écrit
Que de tout inconnu le sage se méfie.

(Fables)

15 enfiler la venelle: prendre la fuite
27 desserre: 'let fly'
28 haut le pied: 'takes to his heels'
29 gâté : 'in a bad way'

Possible comparisons : 7, 17, 63, 70

23

François-Marie Arouet, dit Voltaire, 1694-1778

Les vous et les tu

Philis, qu'est devenu ce temps
Où, dans un fiacre promenée,
Sans laquais, sans ajustements,
De tes grâces seules ornée,
5   Contente d'un mauvais soupé
Que tu changeais en ambroisie,
Tu te livrais, dans ta folie,
A l'amant heureux et trompé
Qui t'avait consacré sa vie?
10   Le ciel ne te donnait alors,
Pour tout rang et pour tous trésors,
Que les agréments de ton âge,
Un cœur tendre, un esprit volage,
Un sein d'albâtre, et de beaux yeux.
15   Avec tant d'attraits précieux,
Hélas! qui n'eût été friponne?
Tu le fus, objet gracieux;
Et (que l'Amour me le pardonne!)
Tu sais que je t'en aimais mieux.
20   Ah, Madame! que votre vie,
D'honneurs aujourd'hui si remplie,
Diffère de ces doux instants!
Ce large suisse à cheveux blancs,
Qui ment sans cesse à votre porte,
25   Philis, est l'image du Temps:
On dirait qu'il chasse l'escorte
Des tendres Amours et des Ris;
Sous vos magnifiques lambris
Ces enfants tremblent de paraître.
30   Hélas! je les ai vus jadis
Entrer chez toi par la fenêtre
Et se jouer dans ton taudis.
        Non, Madame, tous ces tapis
Qu'a tissus la Savonnerie,
35   Ceux que les Persans ont ourdis,
Et toute votre orfèvrerie,
Et ces plats si chers que Germain
A gravés de sa main divine,
Et ces cabinets où Martin
40   A surpassé l'art de Chine;

Vos vases japonais et blancs,
Toutes ces fragiles merveilles;
Ces deux lustres de diamants
Qui pendent à vos deux oreilles;
45 Ces riches carcans, ces colliers,
Et cette pompe enchanteresse,
Ne valent pas un des baisers
Que tu donnais dans ta jeunesse.

Possible comparisons: 1, 13, 14, 80

Evariste de Parny, 1753-1814

Projet de Solitude

Fuyons ces tristes lieux, ô maîtresse adorée!
Nous perdons en espoir la moitié de nos jours,
Et la crainte importune y trouble nos amours.
Non loin de ce rivage est une île ignorée,
5   Interdite aux vaisseaux, et d'écueils entourée.
Un zéphyr éternel y rafraîchit les airs.
Libre et nouvelle encor, la prodigue nature
Embellit de ses dons ce point de l'univers:
Des ruisseaux argentés roulent sur la verdure,
10   Et vont en serpentant se perdre au sein des mers;
Une main favorable y reproduit sans cesse
L'ananas parfumé des plus douces odeurs;
Et l'oranger touffu, courbé sous sa richesse,
Se couvre en même temps et de fruits et de fleurs.
15   Que nous faut-il de plus? Cette île fortunée
Semble par la nature aux amants destinée.
L'océan la resserre, et deux fois en un jour
De cet asile étroit on achève le tour.
Là, je ne craindrai plus un père inexorable;
20   C'est là qu'en liberté tu pourras être aimable,
Et couronner l'amant qui t'a donné son cœur.
Vous coulerez alors, mes paisibles journées,
Par les nœuds du plaisir l'une à l'autre enchaînées:
Laissez-moi peu de gloire et beaucoup de bonheur.
25   Viens; la nuit est obscure et le ciel sans nuage;
D'un éternel adieu saluons ce rivage,
Où par toi seule encor mes pas sont retenus.
Je vois à l'horizon l'étoile de Vénus:
Vénus dirigera notre course incertaine.
30   Eole exprès pour nous vient d'enchaîner les vents;
Sur les flots aplanis Zéphire souffle à peine;
Viens; l'Amour jusqu'au bord conduira deux amants.

(Poèmes érotiques)

Possible comparisons: VIb, 25, 38, 76, 77

22

André Chénier, 1762-1794

Néère

Mais telle qu'à sa mort, pour la dernière fois,
Un beau cygne soupire, et de sa douce voix,
De sa voix qui bientôt lui doit être ravie,
Chante, avant de partir, ses adieux à la vie:
5   Ainsi, les yeux remplis de langueur et de mort,
Pâle, elle ouvrit sa bouche en un dernier effort:
"– O vous, du Sébéthus Naïades vagabondes,
Coupez sur mon tombeau vos chevelures blondes.
Adieu, mon Clinias! moi, celle qui te plus,
10   Moi, celle qui t'aimai, que tu ne verras plus.
O cieux, ô terre, ô mer, prés, montagnes, rivages,
Fleurs, bois mélodieux, vallons, grottes sauvages,
Rappelez-lui souvent, rappelez-lui toujours
Néère, tout son bien, Néère ses amours;
15   Cette Néère, hélas, qu'il nommait sa Néère,
Qui pour lui criminelle, abandonna sa mère;
Qui pour lui fugitive, errant de lieux en lieux,
Aux regards des humains n'osa lever les yeux.
O! soit que l'astre pur des deux frères d'Hélène
20   Calme sous ton vaisseau la vague ionienne,
Soit qu'aux bords de Pæstum, sous ta soigneuse main,
Les roses deux fois l'an couronnent ton jardin,
Au coucher du soleil, si ton âme attendrie
Tombe en une muette et molle rêverie,
25   Alors, mon Clinias, appelle, appelle-moi,
Je viendrai, Clinias, je volerai vers toi.
Mon âme vagabonde, à travers le feuillage,
Frémira. Sur les vents ou sur quelque nuage
Tu la verras descendre, ou du sein de la mer,
30   S'élevant comme un songe, étinceler dans l'air;
Et ma voix, toujours tendre et doucement plaintive
Caresser, en fuyant, ton oreille attentive."

(Bucoliques)

7   Sébéthus: a river in Campagna.

19   soit que l'astre pur . . . : a reference to the constellation and
astrological sign of Gemini, supposedly favourable to sailors.

21   Pæstum: a town near Naples.

Possible comparisons: I, 25, 31

André Chénier, 1762-1794

'Nymphe tendre et vermeille'

Nymphe tendre et vermeille, ô jeune Poésie,
Quel bois est aujourd'hui ta retraite choisie?
Quelles fleurs, près d'une onde où s'égarent tes pas,
Se courbent mollement sous tes pieds délicats?
5 Où te faut-il chercher? Vois la saison nouvelle.
Sur son visage blanc quelle pourpre étincelle!
L'hirondelle a chanté. Zéphire est de retour.
Il revient en dansant. Il ramène l'amour.
L'ombre, les prés, les fleurs. C'est sa douce famille.
10 Et Jupiter se plaît à contempler sa fille,
Cette terre où partout, sous tes doigts gracieux,
S'empressent de germer des vers mélodieux.
Le fleuve qui s'étend dans les vallons humides
Roule pour toi des vers doux, sonores, liquides.
15 Des vers, s'ouvrant en foule aux regards du soleil,
Sont ce peuple de fleurs au calice vermeil.
Et les monts, en torrents qui blanchissent leurs cimes,
Lancent des vers brillants dans le fond des abîmes.

Possible comparisons : VIa, 13, 52, 57, 62, 75

André Chénier, 1762-1794

Iambes XI

Comme un dernier rayon, comme un dernier zéphyre
    Anime la fin d'un beau jour,
Au pied de l'échafaud j'essaye encor ma lyre.
    Peut-être est-ce bientôt mon tour;
5   Peut-être avant que l'heure en cercle promenée
    Ait posé sur l'émail brillant,
Dans les soixante pas où sa route est bornée,
    Son pied sonore et vigilant,
Le sommeil du tombeau pressera ma paupière;
10   Avant que de ses deux moitiés
Ce vers que je commence ait atteint la dernière,
    Peut-être en ces murs effrayés
Le messager de mort, noir recruteur des ombres,
    Escorté d'infâmes soldats,
15   Ebranlant de mon nom ces longs corridors sombres,
    Où seul dans la foule à grands pas
J'erre, aiguisant ces dards persécuteurs du crime,
    Du juste trop faibles soutiens,
Sur mes lèvres soudain va suspendre la rime;
20   Et chargeant mes bras de liens,
Me traîner, amassant en foule à mon passage
    Mes tristes compagnons reclus,
Qui me connaissaient tous avant l'affreux message,
    Mais qui ne me connaissent plus.
25   Eh bien! j'ai trop vécu. Quelle franchise auguste,
    De mâle constance et d'honneur,
Quels exemples sacrés, doux à l'âme du juste,
    Pour lui quelle ombre de bonheur,
Quelle Thémis terrible aux têtes criminelles,
30   Quels pleurs d'une noble pitié,
Des antiques bienfaits quels souvenirs fidèles,
    Quels beaux échanges d'amitié,
Font digne de regrets l'habitacle des hommes?
    La peur fugitive est leur dieu,
35   La bassesse, la feinte. Ah! lâches que nous sommes
    Tous, oui, tous. Adieu, terre, adieu.
Vienne, vienne la mort! Que la mort me délivre!
    Ainsi, donc, mon cœur abattu
Cède au poids de ces maux? Non, non, puissé-je vivre!
40   Ma vie importe à la vertu;

Car l'honnête homme enfin, victime de l'outrage,
Dans les cachots, près du cercueil,
Relève plus altiers son front et son langage,
Brillants d'un généreux orgueil.
45   S'il est écrit aux cieux que jamais une épée
N'étincellera dans mes mains,
Dans l'encre et l'amertume une autre arme trempée
Peut encor servir les humains.
Justice, Vérité, si ma main, si ma bouche,
50   Si mes pensers les plus secrets
Ne froncèrent jamais votre sourcil farouche,
Et si les infâmes progrès,
Si la risée atroce, ou, plus atroce injure,
L'encens de hideux scélérats
55   Ont pénétré vos cœurs d'une longue blessure,
Sauvez-moi; conservez un bras
Qui lance votre foudre, un amant qui vous venge.
Mourir sans vider mon carquois!
Sans percer, sans fouler, sans pétrir dans leur fange
60   Ces bourreaux barbouilleurs de lois!
Ces vers cadavéreux de la France asservie,
Egorgée! O mon cher trésor,
O ma plume! fiel, bile, horreur, dieux de ma vie!
Par vous seuls je respire encor:
65   Comme la poix brûlante agitée en ses veines
Ressuscite un flambeau mourant,
Je souffre, mais je vis. Par vous, loin de mes peines,
D'espérance un vaste torrent
Me transporte. Sans vous, comme un poison livide,
70   L'invisible dent du chagrin,
Mes amis opprimés, du menteur homicide
Le succès, le sceptre d'airain;
Des bons proscrits par lui la mort ou la ruine,
L'opprobre de subir sa loi,
75   Tout eût tari ma vie; ou contre ma poitrine
Dirigé mon poignard. Mais quoi!
Nul ne resterait donc pour attendrir l'histoire
Sur tant de justes massacrés?
Pour consoler leurs fils, leurs veuves, leur mémoire,
80   Pour que des brigands abhorrés
Frémissent aux portraits noirs de leur ressemblance?
Pour descendre jusqu'aux enfers
Nouer le triple fouet, le fouet de la vengeance,
Déjà levé sur ces pervers?
85   Pour cracher sur leurs noms, pour chanter leur supplice?

Allons, étouffe tes clameurs;
Souffre, ô cœur gros de haine, affamé de justice.
Toi, Vertu, pleure, si je meurs.

(Iambes)

3   au pied de l'échafaud : the poem was written while Chénier was in the prison of Saint-Lazare, expecting to be tried and executed at any time.

29   Thémis : the goddess of justice

Possible comparisons: I, 42, 79, 83

Alphonse de Lamartine, 1790-1869

Le Lac

Ainsi, toujours poussés vers de nouveaux rivages,
Dans la nuit éternelle emportés sans retour,
Ne pourrons nous jamais sur l'océan des âges
4   Jeter l'ancre un seul jour?

O lac! l'année à peine a fini sa carrière,
Et près des flots chéris qu'elle devait revoir
Regarde! je viens seul m'asseoir sur cette pierre
8   Où tu la vis s'asseoir!

Tu mugissais ainsi sous ces roches profondes;
Ainsi tu te brisais sur leurs flancs déchirés:
Ainsi le vent jetait l'écume de tes ondes
12   Sur ses pieds adorés.

Un soir, t'en souvient-il? nous voguions en silence;
On n'entendait au loin, sur l'onde et sous les cieux,
Que le bruit des rameurs qui frappaient en cadence
16   Tes flots harmonieux.

Tout à coup des accents inconnus à la terre
Du rivage charmé frappèrent les échos;
Le flot fut attentif, et la voix qui m'est chère
20   Laissa tomber ces mots:

"O temps, suspends ton vol! et vous, heures propices,
Suspendez votre cours!
Laissez-nous savourer les rapides délices
24   Des plus beaux de nos jours!

"Assez de malheureux ici-bas vous implorent:
Coulez, coulez pour eux;
Prenez avec leurs jours les soins qui les dévorent;
28   Oubliez les heureux.

"Mais je demande en vain quelques moments encore,
Le temps m'échappe et fuit;
Je dis à cette nuit: "Sois plus lente"; et l'aurore
32   Va dissiper la nuit.

"Aimons donc, aimons donc! de l'heure fugitive,
Hâtons-nous, jouissons!
L'homme n'a point de port, le temps n'a point de rive;
36   Il coule, et nous passons!"

Temps jaloux, se peut-il que ces moments d'ivresse,
Où l'amour à longs flots nous verse le bonheur,
S'envolent loin de nous de la même vitesse
40   Que les jours de malheur?

Hé quoi! n'en pourrons-nous fixer au moins la trace?
Quoi! passés pour jamais? quoi! tout entiers perdus?
Ce temps qui les donna, ce temps qui les efface,
44   Ne nous les rendra plus?

Eternité, néant, passé, sombres abîmes,
Que faites-vous des jours que vous engloutissez?
Parlez; nous rendrez-vous ces extases sublimes
48   Que vous nous ravissez?

O lac! rochers muets! grottes! forêt obscure!
Vous que le temps épargne ou qu'il peut rajeunir,
Gardez de cette nuit, gardez, belle nature,
52   Au moins le souvenir!

Qu'il soit dans ton repos, qu'il soit dans tes orages,
Beau lac, et dans l'aspect de tes riants coteaux,
Et dans ces noirs sapins, et dans ces rocs sauvages
56   Qui pendent sur tes eaux!

Qu'il soit dans le zéphyr qui frémit et qui passe,
Dans les bruits de tes bords par tes bords répétés,
Dans l'astre au front d'argent qui blanchit ta surface
60   De ses molles clartés!

Que le vent qui gémit, le roseau qui soupire,
Que les parfums légers de ton air embaumé,
Que tout ce qu'on entend, l'on voit ou l'on respire,
64   Tout dise: "Ils ont aimé!"

(Méditations poétiques)

5   The poem relates to the poet's return to the lake he had
previously visited with his beloved, now dying of tuberculosis.

Possible comparisons: 8, 21, 22, 27, 31, 34, 38, 74, 76

Alfred de Vigny, 1797-1863

La Mort du Loup

I

Les nuages couraient sur la lune enflammée
Comme sur l'incendie on voit fuir la fumée,
Et les bois étaient noirs jusques à l'horizon.
Nous marchions sans parler dans l'humide gazon,
5   Dans la bruyère épaisse, et dans les hautes brandes,
Lorsque, sous les sapins pareils à ceux des landes,
Nous avons aperçu les grands ongles marqués
Par les loups voyageurs que nous avons traqués.
Nous avons écouté, retenant notre haleine
10   Et le pas suspendu. - Ni le bois ni la plaine
Ne poussait un soupir dans les airs; seulement
La girouette en deuil criait an firmament;
Car le vent, élevé bien au-dessus des terres,
N'effleurait de ses pieds que les tours solitaires,
15   Et les chênes d'en bas, contre les rocs penchés,
Sur leurs coudes semblaient endormis et couchés.
Rien ne bruissait donc, lorsque, baissant la tête,
Le plus vieux des chasseurs qui s'était mis en quête
A regardé le sable en s'y couchant; bientôt,
20   Lui que jamais ici l'on ne vit en défaut,
A déclaré tout bas que ces marques récentes
Annonçaient la démarche et les griffes puissantes
De deux grands loups-cerviers et de deux louveteaux.
Nous avons tous alors préparé nos couteaux,
25   Et, cachant nos fusils et leurs lueurs trop blanches,
Nous allions pas à pas en écartant les branches.

Trois s'arrêtent, et moi, cherchant ce qu'ils voyaient,
J'aperçois tout à coup deux yeux qui flamboyaient,
Et je vois au delà quatre formes légères
30   Qui dansaient sous la lune an milieu des bruyères,
Comme font chaque jour, à grand bruit sous nos yeux,
Quand le maître revient, les lévriers joyeux.
Leur forme était semblable, et semblable la danse;
Mais les enfants du Loup se jouaient en silence,
35   Sachant bien qu'à deux pas, ne dormant qu'à demi,
Se couche dans ses murs l'homme, leur ennemi.

Le père était debout, et plus loin, contre un arbre,
Sa louve reposait, comme celle de marbre
Qu'adoraient les Romains, et dont les flancs velus
40   Couvaient les demi-dieux Rémus et Romulus.
Le Loup vient et s'assied, les deux jambes dressées,
Par les ongles crochus dans le sable enfoncées.
Il s'est jugé perdu puisqu'il était surpris,
Sa retraite coupée et tous ses chemins pris,
45   Alors il a saisi dans sa gueule brûlante,
Du chien le plus hardi la gorge pantelante,
Et n'a pas desserré ses mâchoires de fer,
Malgré nos coups de feu, qui traversaient sa chair,
Et nos couteaux aigus qui, comme des tenailles,
50   Se croisaient en plongeant dans ses larges entrailles,
Jusqu'au dernier moment où le chien étranglé,
Mort longtemps avant lui, sous ses pieds a roulé.
Le Loup le quitte alors et puis il nous regarde.
Les couteaux lui restaient au flanc jusqu'à la garde,
55   Le clouaient au gazon tout baigné dans son sang;
Nos fusils l'entouraient en sinistre croissant.
Il nous regarde encore, ensuite il se recouche,
Tout en léchant le sang répandu sur sa bouche,
Et sans daigner savoir comment il a péri,
60   Refermant ses grands yeux, meurt sans jeter un cri.

II

J'ai reposé mon front sur mon fusil sans poudre,
Me prenant à penser, et n'ai pu me résoudre
A poursuivre sa Louve et ses fils qui, tous trois
Avaient voulu l'attendre, et, comme je le crois,
65   Sans ses deux louveteaux, la belle et sombre veuve
Ne l'eût pas laissé seul subir la grande épreuve;
Mais son devoir était de les sauver, afin
De pouvoir leur apprendre à bien souffrir la faim,
Et ne jamais entrer dans le pacte des villes
70   Que l'homme a fait avec les animaux serviles
Qui chassent devant lui, pour avoir le coucher,
Les premiers possesseurs du bois et du rocher.

III

Hélas! ai-je pensé, malgré ce grand nom d'Hommes,
Que j'ai honte de nous, débiles que nous sommes!
75   Comment on doit quitter la vie et tous ses maux,

C'est vous qui le savez, sublimes animaux.
A voir ce que l'on fut sur terre et ce qu'on laisse,
Seul le silence est grand, tout le reste est faiblesse.
- Ah! je t'ai bien compris, sauvage voyageur,
80 Et ton dernier regard m'est allé jusqu'au coeur
Il disait: "Si tu peux, fais que ton âme arrive,
A force de rester studieuse et pensive,
Jusqu'à ce haut degré de stoïque fierté
Où, naissant dans les bois, j'ai tout d'abord monté.
85 Gémir, pleurer, prier est également lâche,
Fais énergiquement ta longue et lourde tâche
Dans la voie où le sort a voulu t'appeler,
Puis, après, comme moi, souffre et meurs sans parler."

(Les Destinées)

23   loup-cervier - normally a lynx, but here literally a wolf that
      pursues deer.

Possible comparisons: 17, 18, 19, 38, 68

Victor Hugo, 1802-1885

Soleils couchants, VI

Le soleil s'est couché ce soir dans les nuées.
Demain viendra l'orage, et le soir, et la nuit:
Puis l'aube, et ses clartés de vapeur obstruées:
4   Puis les nuits, puis les jours, pas du temps qui s'enfuit.

Tous ces jours passeront, ils passeront en foule
Sur la face des mers, sur la face des monts,
Sur les fleuves d'argent, sur les forêts où roule
8   Comme un hymne confus des morts que nous aimons.

Et la face des eaux et le front des montagnes,
Ridés et non vieillis, et les bois toujours verts
S'iront rajeunissant: le fleuve des campagnes
12   Prendra sans cesse aux monts le flot qu'il donne aux mers.

Mais moi, sous chaque jour courbant plus bas ma tête,
Je passe, et, refroidi sous ce soleil joyeux,
Je m'en irai bientôt, au milieu de la fête,
16   Sans que rien manque au monde immense et radieux!

22 avril 1829
(*Les Feuilles d'Automne*)

Possible comparisons: VIa, 8, 10, 25

Victor Hugo, 1802–1885

Le Manteau impérial

Oh! vous dont le travail est joie,
Vous qui n'avez pas d'autre proie
Que les parfums, souffles du ciel,
Vous qui fuyez quand vient décembre,
Vous qui dérobez aux fleurs l'ambre
6   Pour donner aux hommes le miel,

Chastes buveuses de rosée,
Qui, pareilles à l'épousée,
Visitez le lys du coteau,
O sœurs de corolles vermeilles,
Filles de la lumière, abeilles,
12   Envolez-vous de ce manteau!

Ruez-vous sur l'homme, guerrières!
O généreuses ouvrières,
Vous le devoir, vous la vertu,
Ailes d'or et flèche de flamme,
Tourbillonnez sur cet infâme!
18   Dites-lui: "Pour qui nous prends-tu?"

"Maudit! nous sommes les abeilles!
Des chalets ombragés de treilles
Notre ruche orne le fronton;
Nous volons, dans l'azur écloses,
Sur la bouche ouverte des roses
24   Et sur les lèvres de Platon.

"Ce qui sort de la fange y rentre.
Va trouver Tibère en son antre,
Et Charles neuf sur son balcon.
Va! sur ta pourpre il faut qu'on mette,
Non les abeilles de l'Hymette,
30   Mais l'essaim noir de Montfaucon!"

Et percez-le tout ensemble,
Faites honte au peuple qui tremble,
Aveuglez l'immonde trompeur,
Acharnez-vous sur lui, farouches,
Et qu'il soit chassé par les mouches
36   Puisque les hommes en ont peur!

Juin 1853
(*Les Châtiments*)

Title: The imperial mantle worn by Louis Napoléon (Napoléon III) whom Hugo attacked as a usurper and a tyrant, was embroidered with bees, symbolising the industrious activity of the French people. The symbol was originally devised by Napoléon I.

24   Platon: according to the legend, some bees alighted on the lips of the infant Plato, thus granting him the gift of eloquence (honeyed words).

26   Tibère: the tyrannical emperor Tiberius, who spent his last years in retirement from Rome; the idea of his continuing to exert a baleful influence from a cave may be an exaggeration.

27   Charles neuf: according to a now discredited legend, Charles IX took an active part in the massacre of St Bartholomew's Eve (1572), shooting at protestants from his balcony.

30   Montfaucon: site of the gibbet in Paris.

Possible comparisons: 18, 19, 24

Victor Hugo, 1802–1885

La Fête chez Thérèse

La chose fut exquise et fort bien ordonnée.
C'était au mois d'avril, et dans une journée
Si douce, qu'on eût dit qu'amour l'eût faite exprès.
Thérèse la duchesse à qui je donnerais,
5   Si j'étais roi, Paris, si j'étais Dieu, le monde,
Quand elle ne serait que Thérèse la blonde;
Cette belle Thérèse, aux yeux de diamant,
Nous avait conviés dans son jardin charmant.

On était peu nombreux. Le choix faisait la fête.
10   Nous étions tous ensemble et chacun tête à tête.
Des couples pas à pas erraient de tous côtés.
C'étaient les fiers seigneurs et les rares beautés,
Les Amyntas rêvant auprès des Léonores,
Les marquises riant avec les monsignores;
15   Et l'on voyait rôder dans les grands escaliers
Un nain qui dérobait leur bourse aux cavaliers.

A midi, le spectacle avec la mélodie.
Pourquoi jouer Plautus la nuit? La comédie
Est une belle fille et rit mieux au grand jour.
20   Or, on avait bâti, comme un temple d'amour,
Près d'un bassin dans l'ombre habité par un cygne,
Un théâtre en treillage où grimpait une vigne.
Un cintre à claire-voie en anse de panier,
Cage verte où sifflait un bouvreuil prisonnier,
25   Couvrait toute la scène, et sur leurs gorges blanches
Les actrices sentaient errer l'ombre des branches.
On entendait au loin de magiques accords;
Et, tout en haut, sortant de la frise à mi-corps,
Pour attirer la foule aux lazzis qu'il répète,
30   Le blanc Pulcinella sonnait de la trompette.

Deux faunes soutenaient le manteau d'Arlequin;
Trivelin leur riait au nez comme un faquin.
Parmi les ornements sculptés dans le treillage,
Colombine dormait dans un gros coquillage,
35   Et, quand elle montrait son sein et ses bras nus,
On eût cru voir la conque, et l'on eût dit Vénus.
Le seigneur Pantalon, dans une niche, à droite,
Vendait des limons doux sur une table étroite,

Et criait par instants : – Seigneurs, l'homme est divin.
40 Dieu n'avait fait que l'eau, mais l'homme a fait le vin –!
Scaramouche en un coin harcelait de sa batte
Le tragique Alcantor, suivi du triste Arbate;
Crispin, vêtu de noir, jouait de l'éventail;
Perché, jambe pendante, au sommet du portail,
45 Carlino se penchait, écoutant les aubades,
Et son pied ébauchait de rêveuses gambades.

Le soleil tenait lieu de lustre; la saison
Avait brodé de fleurs un immense gazon,
Vert tapis déroulé sous maint groupe folâtre.
50 Rangés des deux côtés de l'agreste théâtre,
Les vrais arbres du parc, les sorbiers, les lilas,
Les ébéniers qu'avril charge de falbalas,
De leur sève embaumée exhalant les délices,
Semblaient se divertir à faire les coulisses,
55 Et, pour nous voir, ouvrant leurs fleurs comme des yeux,
Joignaient aux violons leur murmure joyeux;
Si bien qu'à ce concert gracieux et classique,
La nature mêlait un peu de sa musique.

Tout nous charmait, les bois, le jour serein, l'air pur,
60 Les femmes tout amour et le ciel tout azur.

Pour la pièce, elle était fort bonne, quoique ancienne.
C'était, nonchalamment assis sur l'avant-scène,
Pierrot qui haranguait, dans un grave entretien,
Un singe timbalier à cheval sur un chien.
65 Rien de plus. C'était simple et beau. – Par intervalles,
Le singe faisait rage et cognait ses timbales;
Puis Pierrot répliquait. – Ecoutait qui voulait.

L'un faisait apporter des glaces au valet;
L'autre, galant drapé d'une cape fantasque,
70 Parlait bas à sa dame en lui nouant son masque;
Trois marquis attablés chantaient une chanson.
Thérèse était assise à l'ombre d'un buisson;
Les roses pâlissaient à côté de sa joue,
Et, la voyant si belle, un paon faisait la roue.
75 Moi, j'écoutais, pensif, un profane couplet
Que fredonnait dans l'ombre un abbé violet.

La nuit vint; tout se tut; les flambeaux s'éteignirent;
Dans les bois assombris les sources se plaignirent;
Le rossignol, caché dans son nid ténébreux,
80 Chanta comme un poète et comme un amoureux.

Chacun se dispersa sous les profonds feuillages;
Les folles en riant entraînèrent les sages;
L'amante s'en alla dans l'ombre avec l'amant;
Et, troublés comme on l'est en songe, vaguement,
85   Ils sentaient par degrés se mêler à leur âme,
A leurs discours secrets, à leurs regards de flamme,
A leur cœur, à leurs sens, à leur molle raison,
Le clair de lune bleu qui baignait l'horizon.

avril 18 . . .

(*Les Contemplations*)

13   Amyntas, Léonores: names recalling the Italian pastoral literature of the sixteenth and seventeenth centuries. The majority of the figures in the scene that follows are characters (or, in the case of Carlino, an actor) in the Italian *commedia dell'arte* or related forms of French comedy.

42   Alcantor: character in Molière's *Le Mariage Forcé*; the role includes an element of *mock* tragedy.

Arbate: confidant of Mithridate in Racine's tragedy *Mithridate*.

Possible comparisons: 13, 32

Victor Hugo, 1802–1885

'Viens! une flûte invisible'

Viens! une flûte invisible
Soupire dans les vergers. –
La chanson la plus paisible
4   Est la chanson des bergers.

Le vent ride, sous l'yeuse,
Le sombre miroir des eaux. –
La chanson la plus joyeuse
8   Est la chanson des oiseaux.

Que nul soin ne te tourmente.
Aimons-nous! aimons toujours! –
La chanson la plus charmante
12   Est la chanson des amours.

Les Metz, août 18 . . .
(*Les Contemplations*)

Possible comparisons: 34, 48, 49, 50

Victor Hugo, 1802-1885

Mors

Je vis cette faucheuse. Elle était dans son champ.
Elle allait à grands pas moissonnant et fauchant,
Noir squelette laissant passer le crépuscule.
Dans l'ombre où l'on dirait que tout tremble et recule,
5   L'homme suivait des yeux les lueurs de la faux.
Et les triomphateurs sous les arcs triomphaux
Tombaient; elle changeait en désert Babylone,
Le trône en échafaud et l'échafaud en trône,
Les roses en fumier, les enfants en oiseaux,
10   L'or en cendre, et les yeux des mères en ruisseaux.
Et les femmes criaient: – Rends-nous ce petit être.
Pour le faire mourir, pourquoi l'avoir fait naître? –
Ce n'était qu'un sanglot sur terre, en haut, en bas;
Des mains aux doigts osseux sortaient des noirs grabats;
15   Un vent froid bruissait dans les linceuls sans nombre;
Les peuples éperdus semblaient sous la faux sombre
Un troupeau frissonnant qui dans l'ombre s'enfuit;
Tout était sous ses pieds deuil, épouvante et nuit.
Derrière elle, le front baigné de douces flammes,
20   Un ange souriant portait la gerbe d'âmes.

(*Les Contemplations*)

Title: *mors* is the Latin word for death.

Possible comparisons: 10, 25, 35, 42

Gérard de Nerval, 1808-1855

Fantaisie

Il est un air pour qui je donnerais
Tout Rossini, tout Mozart et tout Weber,
Un air très-vieux, languissant et funèbre,
4   Qui pour moi seul a des charmes secrets!

Or chaque fois que je viens à l'entendre,
De deux cents ans mon âme rajeunit . . .
C'est sous Louis treize; et je crois voir s'étendre
8   Un coteau vert, que le couchant jaunit,

Puis un château de brique à coins de pierre,
Aux vitraux teints de rougeâtres couleurs,
Ceint de grands parcs, avec une rivière
12   Baignant ses pieds, qui coule entre des fleurs;

Puis une dame, à sa haute fenêtre,
Blonde aux yeux noirs, en ses habits anciens,
Que, dans une autre existence peut-être,
16   J'ai déjà vue . . . et dont je me souviens!

(*Odelettes*)

Possible comparisons: 34, 35, 52, 72

Gérard de Nerval, 1808–1855

Artémis

La Treizième revient . . . C'est encor la première;
Et c'est toujours la Seule, – ou c'est le seul moment:
Car es-tu Reine, ô toi! la première ou dernière?
4   Es-tu Roi, toi le Seul ou le dernier amant? . . .

Aimez qui vous aima du berceau dans la bière;
Celle que j'aimai seul m'aime encor tendrement:
C'est la Mort – ou la Morte . . . O délice! ô tourment!
8   La rose qu'elle tient, c'est la *Rose trémière.*

Sainte Napolitaine aux mains pleines de feux,
Rose au cœur violet, fleur de sainte Gudule:
As-tu trouvé ta croix dans le désert des Cieux?

12   Roses blanches, tombez! vous insultez nos dieux!
Tombez, fantômes blancs, de votre ciel qui brûle:
– La Sainte de l'abîme est plus sainte à mes yeux!

(*Les Chimères*)

Possible comparisons: 4, 37, 81

Alfred de Musset, 1810–1857

'Quand on perd'

Quand on perd, par triste occurrence,
  Son espérance
  Et sa gaieté
Le remède au mélancolique,
  C'est la musique
6   Et la beauté!

Plus oblige et peut davantage
  Un beau visage
  Qu'un homme armé,
Et rien n'est meilleur que d'entendre
  Air doux et tendre
12   Jadis aimé!

(*Poésies nouvelles*)

Possible comparisons: 25, 30, 32, 49

Alfred de Musset, 1810–1857

Derniers Vers

L'heure de ma mort, depuis dix-huit mois,
De tous les côtés sonne à mes oreilles,
Depuis dix-huit mois d'ennuis et de veilles,
4   Partout je la sens, partout je la vois.

Plus je me débats contre ma misère,
Plus s'éveille en moi l'instinct du malheur;
Et dès que je veux faire un pas sur terre,
8   Je sens tout à coup s'arrêter mon cœur.

Ma force à lutter s'use et se prodigue.
Jusqu'à mon repos, tout est un combat;
Et comme un coursier brisé de fatigue,
12   Mon courage éteint chancelle et s'abat.

(*Œuvres posthumes*)

Possible comparisons: I, III, 8, 31, 32, 42, 74

Théophile Gautier, 1811–1872

Le Pot de Fleurs

    Parfois un enfant trouve une petite graine,
    Et tout d'abord, charmé de ses vives couleurs,
    Pour la planter, il prend un pot de porcelaine
4   Orné de dragons bleus et de bizarres fleurs.

    Il s'en va. La racine en couleuvres s'allonge,
    Sort de terre, fleurit et devient arbrisseau;
    Chaque jour, plus avant, son pied chevelu plonge
8   Tant qu'il fasse éclater le ventre du vaisseau.

    L'enfant revient; surpris il voit la plante grasse
    Sur les débris du pot brandir ses verts poignards;
    Il la veut arracher, mais la tige est tenace;
12   Il s'obstine, et ses doigts s'ensanglantent aux dards.

    Ainsi germa l'amour dans mon âme surprise;
    Je croyais ne semer qu'une fleur de printemps:
    C'est un grand aloès dont la racine brise
16   Le pot de porcelaine aux dessins éclatants.

(Poésies diverses)

Possible comparisons: 4, 7, 13, 47, 67, 69

Théophile Gautier, 1811–1872

Le Spectre de la Rose

Soulève ta paupière close
Qu'effleure un songe virginal;
Je suis le spectre d'une rose
Que tu portais hier au bal.
Tu me pris encore emperlée
Des pleurs d'argent de l'arrosoir,
Et parmi la fête étoilée
8   Tu me promenas tout le soir.

O toi qui de ma mort fus cause,
Sans que tu puisses le chasser,
Toute la nuit mon spectre rose
A ton chevet viendra danser.
Mais ne crains rien, je ne réclame
Ni messe ni *De profundis*;
Ce léger parfum est mon âme,
16   Et j'arrive du paradis.

Mon destin fut digne d'envie:
Pour avoir un trépas si beau,
Plus d'un aurait donné sa vie,
Car j'ai ta gorge pour tombeau,
Et sur l'albâtre où je repose
Un poète avec un baiser
Ecrivit: Ci-gît une rose
24   Que tous les rois vont jalouser.

(*Poésies diverses*)

14   *De profundis*: the opening words of the penitential psalm *De profundis clamavi* (Out of the depths have I cried), used in prayers for the dead.

Possible comparisons: 4, 33

38

Leconte de Lisle, 1818-1894

Midi

Midi, roi des étés, épandu sur la plaine,
Tombe en nappes d'argent des hauteurs du ciel bleu.
Tout se tait. L'air flamboie et brûle sans haleine;
4   La terre est assoupie en sa robe de feu.

L'étendue est immense, et les champs n'ont point d'ombre,
Et la source est tarie où buvaient les troupeaux;
La lointaine forêt, dont la lisière est sombre,
8   Dort là-bas, immobile, en un pesant repos.

Seuls, les grands blés mûris, tels qu'une mer dorée,
Se déroulent au loin, dédaigneux du sommeil;
Pacifiques enfants de la terre sacrée,
12   Ils épuisent sans peur la coupe du soleil.

Parfois, comme un soupir de leur âme brûlante,
Du sein des épis lourds qui murmurent entre eux,
Une ondulation majestueuse et lente
16   S'éveille, et va mourir à l'horizon poudreux.

Non loin, quelques bœufs blancs, couchés parmi les herbes,
Bavent avec lenteur sur leurs fanons épais,
Et suivent de leurs yeux languissants et superbes
20   Le songe intérieur qu'ils n'achèvent jamais.

Homme, si, le cœur plein de joie ou d'amertume,
Tu passais vers midi dans les champs radieux,
Fuis! La nature est vide et le soleil consume:
24   Rien n'est vivant ici, rien n'est triste ou joyeux.

Mais si, désabusé des larmes et du rire,
Altéré de l'oubli de ce monde agité,
Tu veux, ne sachant plus pardonner ou maudire,
28   Goûter une suprême et morne volupté,

Viens! Le soleil te parle en paroles sublimes;
Dans sa flamme implacable absorbe-toi sans fin;
Et retourne à pas lents vers les cités infimes,
32   Le cœur trempé sept fois dans le néant divin.

(Poèmes antiques)

32   néant divin: the Buddhist state of *Nirvana*.

Possible comparisons: VIa, VIb, 13, 21, 25, 26

Charles Baudelaire, 1821-1867

Bohémiens en voyage

La tribu prophétique aux prunelles ardentes
Hier s'est mise en route, emportant ses petits
Sur son dos, ou livrant à leurs fiers appétits
4   Le trésor toujours prêt des mamelles pendantes.

Les hommes vont à pied sous leurs armes luisantes
Le long des chariots où les leurs sont blottis,
Promenant sur le ciel des yeux appesantis
8   Par le morne regret des chimères absentes.

Du fond de son réduit sablonneux, le grillon,
Les regardant passer, redouble sa chanson;
Cybèle, qui les aime, augmente ses verdures,

12   Fait couler le rocher et fleurir le désert
Devant ces voyageurs, pour lesquels est ouvert
L'empire familier des ténèbres futures.

(*Les Fleurs du Mal*)

Possible comparisons: 53, 55, 57, 59

Charles Baudelaire, 1821-1867

'Je te donne ces vers'

Je te donne ces vers afin que si mon nom
Aborde heureusement aux époques lointaines,
Et fait rêver un soir les cervelles humaines,
4   Vaisseau favorisé par un grand aquilon,

Ta mémoire, pareille aux fables incertaines,
Fatigue le lecteur ainsi qu'un tympanon,
Et par un fraternel et mystique chaînon
8   Reste comme pendue à mes rimes hautaines;

Etre maudit à qui, de l'abîme profond
Jusqu'au plus haut du ciel, rien, hors moi, ne répond!
– O toi qui, comme une ombre à la trace éphémère,

12   Foules d'un pied léger et d'un regard serein
Les stupides mortels qui t'ont jugée amère,
Statue aux yeux de jais, grand ange au front d'airain!

(*Les Fleurs du Mal*)

Possible comparisons: 14

Charles Baudelaire, 1821-1867

Mœsta et Errabunda

Dis-moi, ton cœur parfois s'envole-t-il, Agathe,
Loin du noir océan de l'immonde cité,
Vers un autre océan où la splendeur éclate,
Bleu, clair, profond, ainsi que la virginité?
5   Dis-moi, ton cœur parfois s'envole-t-il, Agathe?

La mer, la vaste mer, console nos labeurs!
Quel démon a doté la mer, rauque chanteuse
Qu'accompagne l'immense orgue des vents grondeurs,
De cette fonction sublime de berceuse?
10   La mer, la vaste mer, console nos labeurs!

Emporte-moi, wagon! enlève-moi, frégate!
Loin, loin! ici la boue est faite de nos pleurs!
– Est-il vrai que parfois le triste cœur d'Agathe
Dise: Loin des remords, des crimes, des douleurs,
15   Emporte-moi, wagon, enlève-moi, frégate?

Comme vous êtes loin, paradis parfumé,
Où sous un clair azur tout n'est qu'amour et joie,
Où tout ce que l'on aime est digne d'être aimé,
Où dans la volupté pure le cœur se noie!
20   Comme vous êtes loin, paradis parfumé!

Mais le vert paradis des amours enfantines,
Les courses, les chansons, les baisers, les bouquets,
Les violons vibrant derrière les collines,
Avec les brocs de vin, le soir, dans les bosquets,
25   – Mais le vert paradis des amours enfantines,

L'innocent paradis, plein de plaisirs furtifs,
Est-il déjà plus loin que l'Inde et que la Chine?
Peut-on le rappeler avec des cris plaintifs,
Et l'animer encor d'une voix argentine,
30   L'innocent paradis plein de plaisirs furtifs?

(*Les Fleurs Du Mal*)

Possible comparisons: 2, 21

42

Charles Baudelaire, 1821-1867

Le Mort Joyeux

Dans une terre grasse et pleine d'escargots
Je veux creuser moi-même une fosse profonde,
Où je puisse à loisir étaler mes vieux os
4   Et dormir dans l'oubli comme un requin dans l'onde.

Je hais les testaments et je hais les tombeaux;
Plutôt que d'implorer une larme du monde,
Vivant, j'aimerais mieux inviter les corbeaux
8   A saigner tous les bouts de ma carcasse immonde.

O vers! noirs compagnons sans oreille et sans yeux,
Voyez venir à vous un mort libre et joyeux;
11   Philosophes viveurs, fils de la pourriture,

A travers ma ruine allez donc sans remords,
Et dites-moi s'il est encor quelque torture
14   Pour ce vieux corps sans âme et mort parmi les morts!

(*Les Fleurs du Mal*)

Possible comparisons: I, VIa, 6, 10, 24, 31, 35

Charles Baudelaire, 1821–1867

Spleen

J'ai plus de souvenirs que si j'avais mille ans.

Un gros meuble à tiroirs encombré de bilans,
De vers, de billets doux, de procès, de romances,
Avec de lourds cheveux roulés dans des quittances,
5   Cache moins de secrets que mon triste cerveau.
C'est une pyramide, un immense caveau,
Qui contient plus de morts que la fosse commune.
– Je suis un cimetière abhorré de la lune,
Où comme des remords se traînent de longs vers
10   Qui s'acharnent toujours sur mes morts les plus chers.
Je suis un vieux boudoir plein de roses fanées,
Où gît tout un fouillis de modes surannées,
Où les pastels plaintifs et les pâles Boucher,
Seuls, respirent l'odeur d'un flacon débouché.

15   Rien n'égale en longueur les boiteuses journées,
Quand sous les lourds flocons des neigeuses années,
L'ennui, fruit de la morne incuriosité,
Prend les proportions de l'immortalité.
– Désormais tu n'es plus, ô matière vivante!
20   Qu'un granit entouré d'une vague épouvante,
Assoupi dans le fond d'un Saharah brumeux;
Un vieux Sphinx ignoré du monde insoucieux,
Oublié sur la carte, et dont l'humeur farouche
Ne chante qu'aux rayons du soleil qui se couche.

(*Les Fleurs du Mal*)

Possible comparisons: 47, 56

Charles Baudelaire, 1821-1867

Any where out of the world
N'importe où hors du monde

Cette vie est un hôpital où chaque malade est possédé du
désir de changer de lit. Celui-ci voudrait souffrir en face du
poêle, et celui-là croit qu'il guérirait à côté de la fenêtre.

5   Il me semble que je serais toujours bien là où je ne suis
pas, et cette question de déménagement en est une que je
discute sans cesse avec mon âme.

"Dis-moi, mon âme, pauvre âme refroidie, que penserais-tu
d'habiter Lisbonne? Il doit y faire chaud, et tu t'y ragaillardirais
comme un lézard. Cette ville est au bord de l'eau; on dit qu'elle
10   est bâtie en marbre, et que le peuple y a une telle haine du
végétal, qu'il arrache tous les arbres. Voilà un paysage selon
ton goût; un paysage fait avec la lumière et le minéral, et le
liquide pour les réfléchir!"

Mon âme ne répond pas.

15   "Puisque tu aimes tant le repos, avec le spectacle du
mouvement, veux-tu venir habiter la Hollande, cette terre
béatifiante? Peut-être te divertiras-tu dans cette contrée dont tu
as souvent admiré l'image dans les musées. Que penserais-tu de
Rotterdam, toi qui aimes les forêts de mâts, et les navires
20   amarrés au pied des maisons?"

Mon âme reste muette.

"Batavia te sourirait peut-être davantage? Nous y
trouverions d'ailleurs l'esprit de l'Europe marié à la beauté
tropicale."

25   Pas un mot. – Mon âme serait-elle morte?

"En es-tu donc venue à ce point d'engourdissement que tu ne
te plaises que dans ton mal? S'il en est ainsi, fuyons vers les pays
qui sont les analogies de la Mort. – Je tiens notre affaire, pauvre
âme! Nous ferons nos malles pour Tornéo. Allons plus loin
30   encore, à l'extrême bout de la Baltique; encore plus loin de la
vie, si c'est possible; installons-nous au pôle. Là le soleil ne frise
qu'obliquement la terre, et les lentes alternatives de la lumière
et de la nuit suppriment la variété et augmentent la monotonie,

cette moitié du néant. Là, nous pourrons prendre de longs
35 bains de ténèbres, cependant que, pour nous divertir, les
aurores boréales nous enverront de temps en temps leurs gerbes
roses, comme des reflets d'un feu d'artifice de l'Enfer!"

"Enfin, mon âme fait explosion, et sagement elle me crie:
"N'importe où! n'importe où! pourvu que ce soit hors de ce
40 monde!"

(Petits poèmes en prose)

29 Tornéo: Tornio, a port on the border between Finland and
Sweden. It is in fact *à l'extrême bout de la Baltique.*

Possible comparisons: 55, 57, 63, 70

José-Maria de Heredia, 1842–1905

Oubli

Le temple est en ruine en haut du promontoire.
Et la Mort a mêlé, dans ce fauve terrain,
Les Déesses de marbre et les Héros d'airain
4   Dont l'herbe solitaire ensevelit la gloire.

Seul, parfois, un bouvier menant ses buffles boire,
De sa conque où soupire un antique refrain
Emplissant le ciel calme et l'horizon marin,
8   Sur l'azur infini dresse sa forme noire.

La Terre maternelle et douce aux anciens Dieux
Fait à chaque printemps, vainement éloquente,
Au chapiteau brisé verdir une autre acanthe;

12   Mais l'Homme indifférent au rêve des aïeux
Ecoute sans frémir, au fond des nuits sereines,
La Mer qui se lamente en pleurant des Sirènes.

(*Les Trophées*)

Possible comparisons: VIb, 15

José-Maria de Heredia, 1842–1905

La Belle Viole

> A vous trouppe légère
> Qui d'aile passagère
> Par le monde volez . . .

A Henry Cros

Joachim du Bellay

Accoudée au balcon d'où l'on voit le chemin
Qui va des bords de Loire aux rives d'Italie,
Sous un pâle rameau d'olive son front plie.
4   La violette en fleur se fanera demain.

La viole que frôle encor sa frêle main
Charme sa solitude et sa mélancolie,
Et son rêve s'envole à celui qui l'oublie
8   En foulant la poussière où gît l'orgueil Romain.

De celle qu'il nommait sa douceur Angevine,
Sur la corde vibrante erre l'âme divine
Quand l'angoisse d'amour étreint son cœur troublé;

12   Et sa voix livre aux vents qui l'emportent loin d'elle,
Et le caresseront peut-être, l'infidèle,
Cette chanson qu'il fit pour un vanneur de blé.

(*Les Trophées*)

Epigraph: see poem 3

2   allusion to Du Bellay's journey from his home in the Loire valley (Anjou: cf. *sa douceur Angevine* in line 9) to Rome, the city which inspired his *Antiquités de Rome* and *Regrets*

3   olive: *Olive* is the name given by Du Bellay to the lady to whom his collection of love poems (in fact entitled *L'Olive*) is addressed. Note that Herédia's *viole* is an anagram of *olive*.

Possible comparisons: 3, 50

Stéphane Mallarmé, 1842-1898

'Las de l'amer repos'

Las de l'amer repos où ma paresse offense
Une gloire pour qui jadis j'ai fui l'enfance
Adorable des bois de roses sous l'azur
Naturel, et plus las sept fois du pacte dur
5   De creuser par veillée une fosse nouvelle
Dans le terrain avare et froid de ma cervelle,
Fossoyeur sans pitié pour la stérilité,
– Que dire à cette Aurore, ô Rêves, visité
Par les roses, quand, peur de ses roses livides,
10   Le vaste cimetière unira les trous vides? –

Je veux délaisser l'Art vorace d'un pays
Cruel, et souriant aux reproches vieillis
Que me font mes amis, le passé, le génie,
Et ma lampe qui sait pourtant mon agonie,
15   Imiter le Chinois au cœur limpide et fin
De qui l'extase pure est de peindre la fin
Sur ses tasses de neige à la lune ravie
D'une bizarre fleur qui parfume sa vie
Transparente, la fleur qu'il a sentie, enfant,
20   Au filigrane bleu de l'âme se greffant.
Et, la mort telle avec le seul rêve du sage,
Serein, je vais choisir un jeune paysage
Que je peindrais encor sur les tasses, distrait.
Une ligne d'azur mince et pâle serait
25   Un lac, parmi le ciel de porcelaine nue,
Un clair croissant perdu par une blanche nue
Trempe sa corne calme en la glace des eaux,
Non loin de trois grands cils d'émeraude, roseaux.

(Poèmes)

Possible comparisons: 36, 43, 51, 56

Stéphane Mallarmé, 1842–1898

'Toute l'âme résumée'

Toute l'âme résumée
Quand lente nous l'expirons
Dans plusieurs ronds de fumée
4   Abolis en d'autres ronds

Atteste quelque cigare
Brûlant savamment pour peu
Que la cendre se sépare
8   De son clair baiser de feu.

Ainsi le chœur des romances
A ta lèvre vole-t-il
Exclus-en si tu commences
12   Le réel parce que vil

Le sens trop précis rature
Ta vague littérature.

(Poésies)

Possible comparisons: 23, 30, 34, 49, 50

Paul Verlaine, 1844–1896

Chanson d'automne

Les sanglots longs
Des violons
        De l'automne
Blessent mon cœur
D'une langueur
6   Monotone.

Tout suffocant
Et blême, quand
        Sonne l'heure,
Je me souviens
Des jours anciens
12   Et je pleure;

Et je m'en vais
Au vent mauvais
        Qui m'emporte
Deça, delà
Pareil à la
18   Feuille morte.

(Poèmes saturniens)

Possible comparisons: III, 16, 30, 34, 56

Paul Verlaine, 1844–1896

A Clymène

Mystiques barcarolles,
Romances sans paroles,
Chère puisque tes yeux,
4   Couleur des cieux,

Puisque ta voix, étrange
Vision qui dérange
Et trouble l'horizon
8   De ma raison,

Puisque l'arome insigne
De ta pâleur de cygne
Et puisque la candeur
12   De ton odeur,

Ah! puisque tout ton être,
Musique qui pénètre,
Nimbes d'anges défunts,
16   Tons et parfums,

A, sur d'almes cadences
En ces correspondances
Induit mon cœur subtil,
20   Ainsi soit-il!

(*Fêtes galantes*)

Possible comparisons: 30, 34, 46

Paul Verlaine, 1844-1896

Sonnet Boiteux

A Ernest Delahaye

Ah! vraiment c'est triste, ah! vraiment ça finit trop mal.
Il n'est pas permis d'être à ce point infortuné.
Ah! vraiment c'est trop la mort du naïf animal
4   Qui voit tout son sang couler sous son regard fané.

Londres fume et crie. O quelle ville de la Bible!
Le gaz flambe et nage et les enseignes sont vermeilles.
Et les maisons dans leur ratatinement terrible
8   Epouvantent comme un sénat de petites vieilles.

Tout l'affreux passé saute, piaule, miaule et glapit
Dans le brouillard rose et jaune et sale des Sohos
Avec des *indeeds* et des *allrights* et des *haôs*.

12   Non vraiment c'est trop un martyre sans espérance,
Non vraiment cela finit trop mal, vraiment c'est triste:
O le feu du ciel sur cette ville de la Bible!

(*Jadis et naguère*)

5   allusion to God's destruction of Sodom to punish the inhabitants for their wickedness (Genesis, ch.XIX, v. 24)

Possible comparisons: 15, 16, 47, 68

Arthur Rimbaud, 1854–1891

Ma Bohème
Fantaisie

Je m'en allais, les poings dans mes poches crevées;
Mon paletot aussi devenait idéal;
J'allais sous le ciel, Muse! et j'étais ton féal;
4   Oh! là là! que d'amours splendides j'ai rêvées!

Mon unique culotte avait un large trou.
– Petit Poucet rêveur, j'égrenais dans ma course
Des rimes. Mon auberge était à la Grande-Ourse.
8   – Mes étoiles au cieux avaient un doux frou-frou.

Et je les écoutais, assis au bord des routes,
Ces bons soirs de septembre où je sentais des gouttes
De rosée à mon front, comme un vin de vigueur;

12   Où, rimant au milieu des ombres fantastiques,
Comme des lyres, je tirais les élastiques
De mes souliers blessés, un pied près de mon cœur!

(Poésies)

Possible comparisons: 13, 32, 39, 75

Arthur Rimbaud, 1854–1891

Les Poètes de sept ans

Et la mère, fermant le livre du devoir,
S'en allait satisfaite et très fière, sans voir,
Dans les yeux bleus et sous le front plein d'éminences,
L'âme de son enfant livrée aux répugnances.

5   Tout le jour il suait d'obéissance; très
Intelligent; pourtant des tics noirs, quelques traits
Semblaient prouver en lui d'âcres hypocrisies.
Dans l'ombre des couloirs aux teintures moisies,
En passant il tirait la langue, les deux poings
10   A l'aine, et dans ses yeux fermés voyait des points.
Une porte s'ouvrait sur le soir: à la lampe
On le voyait, là-haut, qui râlait sur la rampe,
Sur un golfe de jour pendant du toit. L'été
Surtout, vaincu, stupide, il était entêté
15   A se renfermer dans la fraîcheur des latrines:
Il pensait là, tranquille et livrant ses narines.
Quand, lavé des odeurs du jour, le jardinet
Derrière la maison en hiver, s'illunait,
Gisant au pied d'un mur, enterré dans la marne
20   Et pour des visions écrasant son œil darne,
Il écoutait grouiller les galeux espaliers.
Pitié! Ces enfants seuls étaient ses familiers
Qui, chétifs, fronts nus, œil déteignant sur la joue,
Cachant de maigres doigts jaunes et noirs de boue
25   Sous des habits puant la foire et tout vieillots,
Conversaient avec la douceur des idiots!
Et si, l'ayant surpris à des pitiés immondes,
Sa mère s'effrayait; les tendresses, profondes,
De l'enfant se jetaient sur cet étonnement.
30   C'était bon. Elle avait le bleu regard, – qui ment!

A sept ans, il faisait des romans, sur la vie
Du grand désert, où luit la Liberté ravie,
Forêts, soleils, rives, savanes! – Il s'aidait
De journaux illustrés où, rouge, il regardait
35   Des Espagnoles rire, et des Italiennes.
Quand venait, l'œil brun, folle, en robes d'indiennes,
– Huit ans, – la fille des ouvriers d'à côté,
La petite brutale, et qu'elle avait sauté,

Dans un coin, sur son dos, en secouant ses tresses,
40 Et qu'il était sous elle, il lui mordait les fesses,
Car elle ne portait jamais de pantalons;
– Et, par elle meurtri des poings et des talons,
Remportait les saveurs de sa peau dans sa chambre.
Il craignait les blafards dimanches de décembre,
45 Où, pommadé, sur un guéridon d'acajou,
Il lisait une Bible à la tranche vert-chou;
Des rêves l'oppressaient chaque nuit dans l'alcôve.
Il n'aimait pas Dieu; mais les hommes, qu'au soir fauve,
Noirs en blouse, il voyait rentrer dans le faubourg
50 Où les crieurs, en trois roulements de tambour,
Font autour des édits rire et gronder les foules.
– Il rêvait la prairie amoureuse, où des houles
Lumineuses, parfums sains, pubescences d'or,
Font leur remuement calme et prennent leur essor!

55 Et comme il savourait surtout les sombres choses,
Quand dans la chambre nue aux persiennes closes,
Haute et bleue, âcrement prise d'humidité,
Il lisait son roman sans cesse médité,
Plein de lourds ciels ocreux et de forêts noyées,
60 De fleurs de chair aux bois sidérals déployées,
Vertige, écroulements, déroutes et pitié!
– Tandis que se faisait la rumeur du quartier,
En bas, – seul, et couché sur des pièces de toiles
Ecrue, et pressentant violemment la voile!

26 mai 1871
(*Poésies*)

Possible comparisons: 62, 83

54

Arthur Rimbaud, 1854–1891

Bonne pensée du matin

A quatre heures du matin, l'été,
Le sommeil d'amour dure encore.
Sous les bosquets l'aube évapore
4   L'odeur du soir fêté.

Mais là-bas dans l'immense chantier
Vers le soleil des Hespérides,
En bras de chemise, les charpentiers
8   Déjà s'agitent.

Dans leur désert de mousse, tranquilles,
Ils préparent les lambris précieux
Où la richesse de la ville
12   Rira sous de faux cieux.

Ah! pour ces Ouvriers charmants
Sujets d'un roi de Babylone,
Vénus! laisse un peu les Amants,
16   Dont l'âme est en couronne.

    O Reine des Bergers!
Porte aux travailleurs l'eau-de-vie,
Pour que leurs forces soient en paix
20 En attendant le bain dans la mer, à midi.

Mai 1872
(*Derniers vers*)

Possible comparisons: VIb, 30, 81

69

Arthur Rimbaud, 1854–1891

Génie

Il est l'affection et le présent puisqu'il a fait la maison ouverte
à l'hiver écumeux et à la rumeur de l'été, lui qui a purifié les
boissons et les aliments, lui qui est le charme des lieux fuyants
et le délice surhumain des stations. Il est l'affection et l'avenir,
5   la force et l'amour que nous, debout dans les rages et les
ennuis, nous voyons passer dans le ciel de tempête et les
drapeaux d'extase.

Il est l'amour, mesure parfaite et réinventée, raison
merveilleuse et imprévue, et l'éternité: machine aimée des
qualités fatales. Nous avions tous eu l'épouvante de sa
10   concession à la nôtre: ô jouissance de notre santé, élan de nos
facultés, affection égoïste et passion pour lui, lui qui nous aime
pour sa vie infinie . . . . Et nous nous le rappelons et il voyage
. . . Et si l'Adoration s'en va, sonne, sa promesse sonne:
"Arrière ces superstitions, ces anciens corps, ces ménages et ces
15   âges. C'est cette époque-ci qui a sombré!"

Il ne s'en ira pas, il ne redescendra pas d'un ciel, il
n'accomplira pas la rédemption des colères de femmes et des
gaîtés des hommes et de tout ce péché: car c'est fait, lui étant,
et étant aimé.

20   O ses souffles, ses têtes, ses courses; la terrible célérité de la
perfection des formes et de l'action.

O fécondité de l'esprit et immensité de l'univers!

Son corps! Le dégagement rêvé, le brisement de la grâce
croisée de violence nouvelle!

25   Sa vue, sa vue! tous les agenouillages anciens et les peines
relevées à sa suite.

Son jour! l'abolition de toutes souffrances sonores et
mouvantes dans la musique plus intense.

Son pas! les migrations plus énormes que les anciennes
30   invasions.

O lui et nous! l'orgueil plus bienveillant que les charités
perdues.

O monde! et le chant clair des malheurs nouveaux!

Il nous a connus tous et nous a tous aimés. Sachons cette nuit
35   d'hiver, de cap en cap, du pôle tumultueux au château, de la
foule à la plage, de regards en regards, forces et sentiments las, le
héler et le voir, et le renvoyer, et sous les marées et au haut des
déserts de neige, suivre ses vues, ses souffles, son corps, son jour.

(Illuminations)

Possible comparisons: II, 44, 57, 63, 82

Jules Laforgue, 1860-1887

Complainte d'un autre dimanche

C'était un très-au vent d'octobre paysage,
Que découpe, aujourd'hui dimanche, la fenêtre,
Avec sa jalousie en travers, hors d'usage,
Où, sèche, depuis quand! une paire de guêtres
5   Tachant de deux mals blancs ce glabre paysage.

Un couchant mal bâti suppurant du livide;
Le coin d'une buanderie aux tuiles sales;
En plein, le Val-de-Grâce, comme un qui préside;
Cinq arbres en proie à de mesquines rafales
10   Qui marbrent ce ciel crû de bandages livides.

Puis les squelettes de glycines aux ficelles,
En proie à des rafales encor plus mesquines!
O lendemains de noce! ô brides de dentelles!
Montrent-elles assez la corde, ces glycines
15   Recroquevillant leur agonie aux ficelles!

Ah! qu'est-ce que je fais, ici, dans cette chambre!
Des vers. Et puis, après! ô sordide limace!
Quoi! la vie est unique, et toi, sous ce scaphandre,
Tu te racontes sans fin, et tu te ressasses!
20   Seras-tu donc toujours un qui garde la chambre?

Ce fut un bien-au vent d'octobre paysage . . .

Paris, octobre 1884; 22, rue Berthollet
Dimanche, retour de Chevreuse.

(*Les Complaintes*)

Possible comparisons: III, 43, 47, 49, 53, 83

Paul Claudel, 1868-1955

from La Muse qui est la Grâce
Antistrophe I

— Que m'importent toutes vos machines et toutes vos œuvres
d'esclaves et vos livres et vos écritures?

O vraiment fils de la terre! ô pataud aux larges pieds! O
vraiment né pour la charrue, arrachant chaque pied au sillon!

5   Celui-ci était fort bien fait pour être clerc d'étude, grossoyant
la minute et l'expédition.

O sort d'une Immortelle attachée à ce lourd imbécile!

Ce n'est point avec le tour et le ciseau que l'on fait un
homme vivant, mais avec une femme, ce n'est pas avec l'encre
10   et la plume que l'on fait une parole vivante!

Quel compte donc fais-tu des femmes? tout serait trop facile
sans elles. Et moi, je suis une femme entre les femmes!

Je ne suis pas accessible à la raison, tu ne feras point, tu ne
feras point de moi ce que tu veux, mais je chante et je danse!

15   Et je ne veux pas que tu aimes une autre femme que moi,
mais moi seule, car il n'en est pas de si belle que je suis,

Et jamais tu ne seras vieux pour moi, mais toujours plus à
mes yeux jeune et beau, jusque tu sois un immortel avec moi!

O sot, au lieu de raisonner, profite de cette heure d'or!
20   Souris! Comprends, tête de pierre! O face d'âne, apprends le
grand rire divin!

Car je ne suis point pour toujours ici, mais je suis fragile sur
ce sol de la terre avec mes deux pieds qui tâtent,

Comme un homme au fond de l'eau qui le repousse, comme
25   un oiseau qui cherche à se poser, les deux ailes à demi
reployées, comme la flamme sur la mèche!

Vois-moi devant toi pour ce court moment, ta bien-aimée,
avec ce visage qui détruit la mort!

Celui qui a bu seulement plein son écuelle de vin nouveau, il
30   ne connaît plus le créancier et le propriétaire;

Il n'est plus l'époux d'une terre maigre et le colon d'une
femme querelleuse avec quatre filles à la maison;

Mais le voici qui bondit tout nu comme un dieu sur le
théâtre, la tête coiffée de pampres, tout violet et poisseux du pis
35   sucré de la grappe,

Comme un dieu au côté de la thymélé, brandissant la peau d'un petit cochon plein de vin qui est la tête du roi Panthée,

Cependant qu'attendant son tour le chœur des garçons et petites filles aux voix fraîches le regarde en croquant des olives salées!

40

Telle est la vertu de cette boisson terrestre: l'ivrogne peu à peu, plein de gaieté, voit double,

Les choses à la fois comme elles sont et comme elles ne sont pas et les gens commencent à ne pas comprendre ce qu'il dit,

45   La vérité sera-t-elle moins forte que le mensonge?

Ferme les yeux seulement et respire la vie froide! Fi de vous, ô chiches jours terrestres! O noces! ô prémisses de l'esprit! bois de ce vin non fermenté seulement!

Avance-toi et vois l'éternel matin, la terre et la mer sous le soleil du matin, comme quelqu'un qui paraît devant le trône de Dieu!

50

Comme l'enfant Jupiter quand il se tint ébloui sur le seuil de la caverne de Dicté,

Le monde autour de toi, non plus comme un esclave soumis, mais comme l'héritier et comme le fils légitime!

55

Car ce n'est point toi qui es fait pour lui, mais c'est lui qui est fait pour toi!

C'en est fait! pourquoi se roidir davantage et résister

Contre l'évidence de ta joie et contre la véhémence de ce souffle céleste? il faut céder!

60

Triomphe et frappe du pied la terre, car qui s'attache à rien,

C'est qu'il n'en est plus le maître, et foule la terre sous tes pieds comme quelqu'un qui danse!

Ris donc, je le veux, de te voir,

65   Ris, immortel! de te voir parmi ces choses périssables!

Et raille, et regarde ce que tu prenais au sérieux! car elles font semblant d'être là et elles passent,

Et elles font semblant de passer, et elles ne cessent pas d'être là!

70   Et toi, tu es avec Dieu pour toujours!

Pour transformer le monde il n'est pas besoin pour toi de la pioche et de la hache et de la truelle et de l'épée,

Mais il te suffit de le regarder seulement, de ces deux yeux de l'esprit qui voit et qui entend.

(Cinq Grandes Odes)
©Editions Gallimard

33   Un dieu sur le théâtre; Dionysus (Bacchus), god of wine and of irrational inspiration, in whose honour were held the festivals from which Greek drama developed.

36   Thymélé: an altar, especially that which stood in the centre of the *orchestra* in the Greek theatre; the chorus-leader stood on its steps.

37   Panthée: presumably Pentheus, the king who attempted to ban the cult of Dionysus, because of the frenzied and ecstatic rites in which its (predominantly female) devotees engaged. He was torn to pieces by the worshippers of Dionysus, led by his own mother. (The myth is treated in Euripides' *Bacchæ*).

53   Dicté: the mountain in Crete where the infant Jupiter was hidden from his father Saturn, who would have swallowed him to avoid being superseded by him.

Possible comparisons: 44, 55, 68, 75, 82

Paul Valéry, 1871-1945

Les Pas

Tes pas, enfants de mon silence,
Saintement, lentement placés,
Vers le lit de ma vigilance
4   Procèdent muets et glacés.

Personne pure, ombre divine,
Qu'ils sont doux, tes pas retenus!
Dieux . . . tous les dons que je devine
8   Viennent à moi sur ces pieds nus!

Si, de tes lèvres avancées,
Tu prépares pour l'apaiser,
A l'habitant de mes pensées
12   La nourriture d'un baiser,

Ne hâte pas cet acte tendre,
Douceur d'être et de n'être pas,
Car j'ai vécu de vous attendre,
16   Et mon cœur n'était que vos pas.

(*Charmes*)
©Editions Gallimard

Possible comparisons: IV, Vb, 32, 50, 77

Paul Valéry, 1871-1945

Le Rameur
à André Lebey

Penché contre un grand fleuve, infiniment mes rames
M'arrachent à regret aux riants environs;
Ame aux pesantes mains, pleines des avirons,
4   Il faut que le ciel cède au glas des lentes lames.

Le cœur dur, l'œil distrait des beautés que je bats,
Laissant autour de moi mûrir des cercles d'onde,
Je veux à larges coups rompre l'illustre monde
8   De feuilles et de feu que je chante tout bas.

Arbres sur qui je passe, ample et naïve moire,
Eau de ramages peinte, et paix de l'accompli,
Déchire-les, ma barque, impose-leur un pli
12   Qui coure du grand calme abolir ma mémoire.

Jamais, charmes du jour, jamais vos grâces n'ont
Tant souffert d'un rebelle essayant sa défense:
Mais, comme les soleils m'ont tiré de l'enfance,
16   Je remonte à la source où cesse même un nom.

En vain toute la nymphe énorme et continue
Empêche de bras purs mes membres harassés;
Je romprai lentement mille liens glacés
20   Et les barbes d'argent de sa puissance nue.

Ce bruit secret des eaux, ce fleuve étrangement
Place mes jours dorés sous un bandeau de soie;
Rien plus aveuglément n'use l'antique joie
24   Qu'un bruit de fuite égale et de nul changement.

Sous les ponts annelés, l'eau profonde me porte,
Voûtes pleines de vent, de murmure et de nuit,
Ils courent sur un front qu'ils écrasent d'ennui,
28   Mais dont l'os orgueilleux est plus dur que leur porte.

Leur nuit passe longtemps. L'âme baisse sous eux
Ses sensibles soleils et ses promptes paupières,
Quand, par le mouvement qui me revêt de pierres,
32   Je m'enfonce au mépris de tant d'azur oiseux.

(*Charmes*)
©Editions Gallimard

Possible comparisons: 25, 39

60

Guillaume Apollinaire, 1880–1918

Marie

Vous y dansiez petite fille
Y danserez-vous mère-grand
C'est la maclotte qui sautille
Toutes les cloches sonneront
5   Quand donc reviendrez-vous Marie

Les masques sont silencieux
Et la musique est si lointaine
Qu'elle semble venir des cieux
Oui je veux vous aimer mais vous aimer à peine
10   Et mon mal est délicieux

Les brebis s'en vont dans la neige
Flocons de laine et ceux d'argent
Des soldats passent et que n'ai-je
Un cœur à moi ce cœur changeant
15   Changeant et puis encor que sais-je

Sais-je où s'en iront tes cheveux
Crépus comme mer qui moutonne
Sais-je où s'en iront tes cheveux
Et tes mains feuilles de l'automne
20   Que jonchent aussi nos aveux

Je passais au bord de la Seine
Un livre ancien sous le bras
Le fleuve est pareil à ma peine
Il s'écoule et ne tarit pas
25   Quand donc finira la semaine.

(*Alcools*)

3   maclotte: an Alsatian folk-dance

Possible comparisons: Vb, 67, 71, 80

Guillaume Apollinaire, 1880-1918

La nuit d'avril 1915

Le ciel est étoilé par les obus des Boches
La forêt merveilleuse où je vis donne un bal
La mitrailleuse joue un air à triples-croches
Mais avez-vous le mot
      Eh! oui le mot fatal
5 Aux créneaux Aux créneaux Laissez là les pioches

Comme un astre éperdu qui cherche ses saisons
Cœur obus éclaté tu sifflais ta romance
Et tes mille soleils ont vidé les caissons
Que les dieux de mes yeux remplissent en silence

10 Nous vous aimons ô vie et nous vous agaçons

Les obus miaulaient un amour à mourir
Un amour qui se meurt est plus doux que les autres
Ton souffle nage au fleuve où le sang va tarir
Les obus miaulaient
      Entends chanter les nôtres
15 Pourpre amour salué par ceux qui vont périr

Ulysse que de jours pour rentrer dans Ithaque
Couche-toi sur la paille et songe un beau remords
Qui pur effet de l'art soit aphrodisiaque
Mais
    orgues
      aux fétus de la paille où tu dors
20 L'hymne de l'avenir est paradisiaque

(Calligrammes)

Possible comparisons: 72

78

Guillaume Apollinaire, 1880-1918

La jolie rousse

Me voici devant tous un homme plein de sens
Connaissant la vie et de la mort ce qu'un vivant peut connaître
Ayant éprouvé les douleurs et les joies d'amour
Ayant su quelquefois imposer ses idées
5   Connaissant plusieurs langages
Ayant pas mal voyagé
Ayant vu la guerre dans l'Artillerie et l'Infanterie
Blessé à la tête trépané sous le chloroforme
Ayant perdu ses meilleurs amis dans l'effroyable lutte
10   Je sais d'ancien et de nouveau autant qu'un homme seul
          pourrait des deux savoir
Et sans m'inquiéter aujourd'hui de cette guerre
Entre nous et pour nous mes amis
Je juge cette longue querelle de la tradition et de l'invention
          De l'Ordre et de l'Aventure

15   Vous dont la bouche est faite à l'image de celle de Dieu
Bouche qui est l'ordre même
Soyez indulgents quand vous nous comparez
A ceux qui furent la perfection de l'ordre
Nous qui quêtons partout l'aventure
20   Nous ne sommes pas vos ennemis
Nous voulons vous donner de vastes et d'étranges domaines
Où le mystère en fleurs s'offre à qui veut le cueillir
Il y a là des feux nouveaux des couleurs jamais vues
Mille phantasmes impondérables
25   Auxquels il faut donner de la réalité
Nous voulons explorer la bonté contrée énorme où tout se tait
Il y a aussi le temps qu'on peut chasser ou faire revenir
Pitié pour nous qui combattons toujours aux frontières
De l'illimité et de l'avenir
30   Pitié pour nos erreurs pitié pour nos péchés

Voici que vient l'été la saison violente
Et ma jeunesse est morte aussi que le Printemps
O Soleil c'est le temps de la Raison ardente
          Et j'attends
35   Pour la suivre toujours la forme noble et douce
Qu'elle prend afin que je l'aime seulement
Elle vient et m'attire ainsi qu'un fer l'aimant
          Elle a l'aspect charmant
          D'une adorable rousse

40   Ses cheveux sont d'or on dirait
Un bel éclair qui durerait
Ou ces flammes qui se pavanent
Dans les roses-thé qui se fanent

Mais riez riez de moi
45   Hommes de partout surtout gens d'ici
Car il y a tant de choses que je n'ose vous dire
Tant de choses que vous ne me laisseriez pas dire
Ayez pitié de moi

(Calligrammes)

Possible comparisons: 53, 57, 66, 68, 71, 75, 82

Saint-John Perse, 1887–1975

Histoire du Régent

Tu as vaincu! tu as vaincu! Que le sang
était beau, et la main
    qui du pouce et du doigt essuyait une lame! . . .
C'était
5   il y a des lunes. Et nous avions eu chaud. Il me
souvient des femmes qui fuyaient avec des cages
d'oiseaux verts; des infirmes qui raillaient; et
des paisibles culbutés au plus grand lac de ce pays . . .;
du prophète qui courait derrière les palissades, sur
10   une chamelle borgne . . .

    Et tout un soir, autour des feux, on fit ranger
les plus habiles de ceux-là
    qui sur la flûte et le triangle savent tenir un
chant.
15   Et les bûchers croulaient chargés de fruit
humain. Et les Rois couchaient nus dans l'odeur de
la mort. Et quand l'ardeur eut délaissé les cendres
fraternelles,
20   nous avons recueilli les os blancs que voilà,
    baignant dans le vin pur.

(*La Gloire des Rois*)
©Editions Gallimard

Possible comparisons: 18, 19, 44, 55, 70, 78

64

Paul Eluard, 1895-1952

Denise disait aux merveilles

Le soir traînait des hirondelles. Les hiboux
Partageaient le soleil et pesaient sur la terre
Comme les pas jamais lassés d'un solitaire
4   Plus pâle que nature et dormant tout debout.

Le soir traînait des armes blanches sur nos têtes.
Le courage brûlait les femmes parmi nous,
Elles pleuraient, elles criaient comme des bêtes,
8   Les hommes inquiets s'étaient mis à genoux.

Le soir, un rien, une hirondelle qui dépasse,
Un peu de vent, les feuilles qui ne tombent plus,
Un beau détail, un sortilège sans vertus
12   Pour un regard qui n'a jamais compris l'espace.

(*Mourir de ne pas mourir*)
©Editions Gallimard

Possible comparisons: 66, 71

Paul Eluard, 1895–1952

'La terre est bleue comme une orange'

La terre est bleue comme une orange
Jamais une erreur les mots ne mentent pas
Ils ne vous donnent plus à chanter
Au tour des baisers de s'entendre
5   Les fous et les amours
Elle sa bouche d'alliance
Tous les secrets tous les sourires
Et quels vêtements d'indulgence
A la croire toute nue

10   Les guêpes fleurissent vert
L'aube se passe autour du cou
Un collier de fenêtres
Des ailes couvrent les feuilles
Tu as toutes les joies solaires
15   Tout le soleil sur terre
Sur les chemins de ta beauté.

(L'amour la poésie)
©Editions Gallimard

Possible comparisons: 66, 71, 73

André Breton, 1896-1966

Au regard des Divinités

A Louis Aragon

"Un peu avant minuit près du débarcadère.
"Si une femme échevelée te suit n'y prends pas garde.
"C'est l'azur. Tu n'as rien à craindre de l'azur.
"Il y aura un grand vase blond dans un arbre.
5   "Le clocher du village des couleurs fondues
"Te servira de point de repère. Prends ton temps,
"Souviens-toi. Le geyser brun qui lance au ciel les pousses de
        fougère
"Te salue."
          La lettre cachetée aux trois coins d'un poisson
Passait maintenant dans la lumière des faubourgs
10   Comme un enseigne de dompteur.
                  Au demeurant
La belle, la victime, celle qu'on appelait
Dans le quartier la petite pyramide de réséda
Décousait pour elle seule un nuage pareil
A un sachet de pitié.
           Plus tard l'armure blanche
15   Qui vaquait aux soins domestiques et autres
En prenant plus fort à son aise que jamais,
L'enfant à son coquille, celui qui devait être . . .
Mais silence.
        Un brasier déjà donnait prise
En son sein à un ravissant roman de cape
20   Et d'épée.
          Sur le pont, à la même heure,
Ainsi la rosée à tête de chatte se berçait.
La nuit, – et les illusions seraient perdues.

Voici les pères blancs qui reviennent de vêpres
Avec l'immense clé pendue au-dessus d'eux
25   Voici les hérauts gris; enfin voici sa lettre
Ou sa lèvre: mon cœur est un coucou pour Dieu.

Mais le temps qu'elle parle, il ne reste qu'un mur
Battant dans un tombeau comme une voile bise.
L'éternité recherche un montre-bracelet
30   Un peu avant minuit près du débarcadère.

(*Clair de Terre*)
©Editions Gallimard

Possible comparisons: 64, 65, 71, 73

Louis Aragon, 1897–1982

'Il n'y a pas d'amour heureux'

Rien n'est jamais acquis à l'homme Ni sa force
Ni sa faiblesse ni son cœur Et quand il croit
Ouvrir ses bras son ombre est celle d'une croix
Et quand il croit serrer son bonheur il le broie
Sa vie est un étrange et douloureux divorce
6   Il n'y a pas d'amour heureux

Sa vie Elle ressemble à ces soldats sans armes
Qu'on avait habillés pour un autre destin
A quoi peut leur servir de se lever matin
Eux qu'on retrouve au soir désœuvrés incertains
Dites ces mots Ma vie Et retenez vos larmes
12   Il n'y a pas d'amour heureux

Mon bel amour mon cher amour ma déchirure
Je te porte dans moi comme un oiseau blessé
Et ceux-là sans savoir nous regardent passer
Répétant après moi les mots que j'ai tressés
Et qui pour tes grands yeux tout aussitôt moururent
18   Il n'y a pas d'amour heureux

Le temps d'apprendre à vivre il est déjà trop tard
Que pleurent dans la nuit nos cœurs à l'unisson
Ce qu'il faut de malheur pour la moindre chanson
Ce qu'il faut de regrets pour payer un frisson
Ce qu'il faut de sanglots pour un air de guitare
24   Il n'y a pas d'amour heureux

Il n'y a pas d'amour qui ne soit à douleur
Il n'y a pas d'amour dont on ne soit meurtri
Il n'y a pas d'amour dont on ne soit flétri
Et pas plus que de toi l'amour de la patrie
Il n'y a pas d'amour qui ne vive de pleurs
30   Il n'y a pas d'amour heureux
      Mais c'est notre amour à tous deux.

Lyon, janvier 1943
(*La Diane Française*)

©P. Seghers

Possible comparisons: 7, 36, 60, 79, 80

Louis Aragon, 1897–1982

Epilogue

Je me tiens sur le seuil de la vie et de la mort les yeux baissés
    les mains vides
Et la mer dont j'entends le bruit est une mer qui ne rend
    jamais ses noyés
Et l'on voit disperser mon âme après moi vendre à l'encan
    mes rêves broyés
4   Voilà déjà que mes paroles sèchent comme une feuille à
    ma lèvre humide

J'écrirai ces vers à bras grands ouverts qu'on sente mon cœur
    quatre fois y battre
Quitte à en mourir je dépasserai ma gorge et ma voix mon
    souffle et mon chant
Je suis le faucheur ivre de faucher qu'on voit dévaster sa vie et
    son champ
8   Et tout haletant du temps qu'il y perd qui bat et rebat sa faux
    comme plâtre

J'ai choisi de donner à mes vers cette envergure de crucifixion
Et qu'en tombe au hasard la chance n'importe où sur moi le
    couteau des césures
Il me faut bien à la fin des fins atteindre une mesure à ma
    démesure
12   Pour à la taille de la réalité faire un manteau de mes fictions

La vie aura passé comme un grand château triste que tous les
    vents traversent
Les courants d'air claquent les portes et pourtant aucune
    chambre n'est fermée
Il s'y assied des inconnus pauvres et las qui sait pourquoi
    certains armés
16   Les herbes ont poussé dans les fossés si bien qu'on n'en peut
    plus baisser la herse

Dans cette demeure en tout cas anciens ou nouveaux nous ne
    sommes pas chez nous
Personne à coup sûr ne sait ce qui le mène ici tout peut-être
    n'est qu'un songe
Certains ont froid d'autres ont faim la plupart des gens ont un
    secret qui les ronge
20   De temps en temps passent des rois sans visage On se met
    devant eux à genoux

Quand j'étais jeune on me racontait que bientôt viendrait la
victoire des anges
Ah comme j'y ai cru comme j'y ai cru puis voilà que je suis
devenu vieux
Le temps des jeunes gens leur est une mèche toujours
retombant dans les yeux
24 Et ce qu'il en reste aux vieillards est trop lourd et trop court
que pour eux le vent change

Ils s'interrogent sur l'essentiel sur ce qui vaut encore qu'on s'y
voue
Ils voient le peu qu'ils ont fait parcourant ce chantier
monstrueux qu'ils abandonnent
L'ombre préférée à la proie ô pauvres gens l'avenir qui n'est
à personne
28 Petits qui jouez dans la rue enfants quelle pitié sans bornes
j'ai de vous

Je vois tout ce que vous avez devant vous de malheur de
sang de lassitude
Vous n'aurez rien appris de nos illusions rien de nos faux pas
compris
Nous ne vous aurons à rien servi vous devrez à votre tour
payer le prix
32 Je vois se plier votre épaule A votre front je vois le pli
des habitudes

Bien sûr bien sûr vous me direz que c'est toujours comme
cela mais justement
Songez à tous ceux qui mirent leurs doigts vivants leurs
mains de chair dans l'engrenage
Pour que cela change et songez à ceux qui ne discutaient même
pas leur cage
36 Est-ce qu'on peut avoir le droit au désespoir le droit de
s'arrêter un moment

Et vienne un jour quand vous aurez sur vous le soleil insensé de
la victoire
Rappelez-vous que nous avons aussi connu cela que d'autre
sont montés
Arracher le drapeau de servitude à l'Acropole et qu'on les a
jetés
40 Eux et leur gloire encore haletants dans la fosse commune de
l'histoire

Songez qu'on n'arrête jamais de se battre et qu'avoir vaincu
n'est trois fois rien
Et que tout est remis en cause du moment que l'homme de
l'homme est comptable
Nous avons vu faire de grandes choses mais il y en eut
d'épouvantables
44   Car il n'est pas toujours facile de savoir où est le mal et où est
le bien

Vous passerez par où nous passâmes naguère en vous je lis à
livre ouvert
J'entends ce cœur qui bat en vous comme un cœur me
semble-t-il en moi battait
Vous l'userez je sais comment et comment cette chose en vous
s'éteint se tait
48   Comment l'automne se défarde et le silence autour d'une rose
d'hiver

Je ne dis pas cela pour démoraliser Il faut regarder le néant
En face pour savoir en triompher Le chant n'est pas le moins
beau quand il décline
Il faut savoir ailleurs l'entendre qui renaît comme l'écho dans
les collines
52   Nous ne sommes pas seuls au monde à chanter et le drame est
l'ensemble des chants

Le drame il faut savoir y tenir sa partie et même qu'une voix
se taise
Sachez-le toujours le chœur profond reprend la phrase
interrompue
Du moment que jusqu'au bout de lui-même le chanteur a fait
ce qu'il a pu
56   Qu'importe si chemin faisant vous allez m'abandonner comme
une hypothèse

Je vous laisse à mon tour comme le danseur qui se lève une
dernière fois
Ne lui reprochez pas dans ses yeux s'il trahit déjà ce qu'il porte
en lui d'ombre
Je ne peux plus vous faire d'autres cadeaux que ceux de cette
lumière sombre
60   Hommes de demain soufflez sur les charbons A vous de dire ce
que je vois

(Les Poètes)
©Louis Aragon

Possible comparisons: 18, 19, 26, 51, 57, 62

Francis Ponge, 1899–

La Bougie

La nuit ravive parfois une plante singulière dont la lueur décompose les chambres meublées en massifs d'ombre.

Sa feuille d'or tient impassible au creux d'une colonnette d'albâtre par un pédoncule très noir.

5   Les papillons miteux l'assaillent de préférence à la lune trop haute, qui vaporise les bois. Mais brûlés aussitôt ou vannés dans la bagarre, tous frémissent aux bords d'une frénésie voisine de la stupeur.

Cependant la bougie, par le vacillement des clartés sur le 10   livre au brusque dégagement des fumées originales encourage le lecteur, – puis s'incline sur son assiette et se noie dans son aliment.

(*Le parti pris des choses*)
© Editions Gallimard

Possible comparisons: VIb, 36

Henri Michaux, 1899-1984

Les Emanglons
Mœurs et coutumes

Quand un Emanglon respire mal ils préfèrent ne plus le voir
vivre. Car ils estiment qu'il ne peut plus atteindre la vraie joie,
quelque effort qu'il y apporte. Le malade ne peut, par le fait de
la sympathie naturelle aux hommes, qu'apporter du trouble
5   dans la respiration d'une ville entière.
Donc, mais tout à fait sans se fâcher, on l'étouffe.
A la campagne, on est assez fruste, on s'entend à quelques-
uns, et un soir on va chez lui et on l'étouffe.
Ils pénètrent dans la cabane en criant: "Amis!" Ils avancent,
10   serrés les uns contre les autres, les mains tendues. C'est vite
fait. Le malade n'a pas le temps d'être vraiment étonné que déjà
il est étranglé par des mains fortes et décidées, des mains
d'hommes de devoir. Puis ils s'en vont placidement et disent à
qui ils rencontrent: "Vous savez, un tel qui avait le souffle si
15   chaotique, eh bien! soudain il l'a perdu devant nous.
– Ah!" fait-on, et le village retrouve sa paix et sa tranquillité.

Mais dans les villes, il y a pour l'étouffement une cérémonie,
d'ailleurs simple, comme il convient
Pour étouffer, on choisit une belle jeune fille vierge.
20   Grand instant pour elle que d'être appelée ainsi au pont entre
vie et mort! La douceur avec laquelle ces souffrants trépassent
est comptée en faveur de la jeune fille. Car avoir fait qu'un
malade s'éteigne doucement entre des mains agréables, est,
disent-ils, excellent présage de dévouement aux enfants, de
25   charité aux pauvres, et pour les biens, de gestion sûre. Elle
trouve aussitôt bien plus de maris qu'il ne lui en faut, et il lui
est permis de choisir elle-même.
La difficulté est d'être douce à la fois et de serrer fort.
Une coquette ne réussira pas, une brutale non plus. Il faut
30   des qualités de fond, une nature vraiment féminine.
Mais quel bonheur quand on a réussi, et comme on
comprend les larmes de joie de la jeune fille cependant que
l'assistance la félicite avec émotion!

(Ailleurs)
© Editions Gallimard

Possible comparisons: 18, 19, 44, 63, 78

Benjamin Péret, 1899–1959

Clin d'oeil

Des vols de perroquets traversent ma tête quand je te vois de
   profil
et le ciel de graisse se strie d'éclairs bleus
qui tracent ton nom dans tous les sens
Rosa coiffée d'une tribu nègre étagée sur un escalier
5   où les seins aigus des femmes regardent par les yeux des
   hommes
Aujourd'hui je regarde par tes cheveux
Rosa d'opale du matin
et je m'éveille par tes yeux
Rosa d'armure
10   et je pense par tes seins d'explosion
Rosa d'étang verdi par les grenouilles
et je dors dans ton nombril de mer Caspienne
Rosa d'églantine pendant la grève générale
et je m'égare entre tes épaules de voie lactée fécondée par des
   comètes
15   Rosa de jasmin dans la nuit de lessive
Rosa de maison hantée
Rosa de forêt noire inondée de timbres-postes bleus et verts
Rosa de cerf-volant au-dessus d'un terrain vague où se battent
   des enfants
Rosa de fumée de cigare
20   Rosa d'écume de mer faite cristal
Rosa

(Je sublime)
©Le Terrain Vague

Possible comparisons: Va, Vb, 60, 64, 66, 73

Jacques Prévert, 1900-1976

Barbara

Rappelle-toi Barbara
Il pleuvait sans cesse sur Brest ce jour-là
Et tu marchais souriante
Epanouie ravie ruisselante
5 Sous la pluie
Rappelle-toi Barbara
Il pleuvait sans cesse sur Brest
Et je t'ai croisée rue de Siam
Tu souriais
10 Et moi je souriais de même
Rappelle-toi Barbara
Toi que je ne connaissais pas
Toi qui ne me connaissais pas
Rappelle-toi
15 Rappelle-toi quand même ce jour-là
N'oublie pas
Un homme sous un porche s'abritait
Et il a crié ton nom
Barbara
20 Et tu as couru vers lui sous la pluie
Ruisselante ravie épanouie
Et tu t'es jetée dans ses bras
Rappelle-toi cela Barbara
Et ne m'en veux pas si je te tutoie
25 Je dis tu à tous ceux que j'aime
Même si je ne les ai vus qu'une seule fois
Je dis tu à tous ceux qui s'aiment
Même si je ne les connais pas
Rappelle-toi Barbara
30 N'oublie pas
Cette pluie sage et heureuse
Sur ton visage heureux
Sur cette ville heureuse
Cette pluie sur la mer
35 Sur l'arsenal
Sur le bateau d'Ouessant
Oh Barbara
Quelle connerie la guerre
Qu'es-tu devenue maintenant
40 Sous cette pluie de fer

De feu d'acier de sang
Et celui qui te serrait dans ses bras
Amoureusement
Est-il mort disparu ou bien encore vivant
45 Oh Barbara
Il pleut sans cesse sur Brest
Comme il pleuvait avant
Mais ce n'est plus pareil et tout est abîmé
C'est une pluie de deuil terrible et désolée
50 Ce n'est même plus l'orage
De fer d'acier de sang
Tout simplement des nuages
Qui crèvent comme des chiens
Des chiens qui disparaissent
55 Au fil de l'eau sur Brest
Et vont pourrir au loin
Au loin très loin de Brest
Dont il ne reste rien.

(*Paroles*)
©Editions Gallimard

2 Brest: During the Second World War the naval dockyard was taken over by the Germans as a submarine base; the town was badly damaged by Allied bombing.

Possible comparisons: 32, 61

Jacques Prévert, 1900-1976

Inventaire

Une pierre
Deux maisons
trois ruines
quatre fossoyeurs
5   un jardin
des fleurs
un raton laveur

une douzaine d'huîtres un citron un pain
un rayon de soleil
10   une lame de fond
six musiciens
une porte avec son paillasson
un monsieur décoré de la légion d'honneur

un autre raton laveur

15   un sculpteur qui sculpte des Napoléons
la fleur qu'on appelle souci
deux amoureux sur un grand lit
un receveur des contributions une chaise trois dindons
un ecclésiastique un furoncle
20   une guêpe
un rein flottant
une écurie de courses
un fils indigne deux frères dominicains trois sauterelles un
    strapontin
deux filles de joie un oncle Cyprien
25   une Mater dolorosa trois papas gâteau deux chèvres de
    Monsieur Seguin

un talon Louis XV
un fauteuil Louis XVI
un buffet Henri II deux buffets Henri III trois buffets Henri IV
un tiroir dépareillé
30   une pelote de ficelle deux épingles de sûreté un monsieur âgé
une Victoire de Samothrace un comptable deux aides-
    comptables
un homme du monde deux chirurgiens trois végétariens
un cannibale
une expédition coloniale un cheval entier une demi-pinte de
    bon sang une mouche tsé-tsé

<pre>
35   un homard à l'américaine un jardin à la française
          deux pommes à l'anglaise
          un face à main un valet de pied un orphelin un poumon d'acier
          un jour de gloire
          une semaine de bonté
40   un mois de Marie
          une année terrible
          une minute de silence
          une seconde d'inattention
          et . . . .

45   cinq ou six ratons laveurs

          un petit garçon qui entre à l'école en pleurant
          un petit garçon qui sort de l'école en riant
          une fourmi
          deux pierres à briquet
50   dix-sept éléphants un juge d'instruction en vacances assis sur
                un pliant
          un paysage avec beaucoup d'herbe verte dedans
          une vache
          un taureau
          deux belles amours trois grandes orgues un veau marengo
55   un soleil d'Austerlitz
          un siphon d'eau de Seltz
          un vin blanc citron
          un Petit Poucet un grand pardon un calvaire de pierre une
                échelle de corde
          deux sœurs latines trois dimensions douze apôtres mille et une
                nuits trente-deux positions six parties du monde cinq
                points cardinaux dix ans de bons et loyaux services
                sept péchés capitaux deux doigts de la main dix gouttes
                avant chaque repas trente jours de prison dont quinze de
                cellule cinq minutes d'entr'acte

          et . . .

60   plusieurs ratons laveurs
</pre>

(Paroles)
©Editions Gallimard

25   mater dolorosa: (Latin: *sorrowing mother*): an artistic
          representation (picture, statuette, etc) of the Virgin at the foot
          of the Cross

26   chèvre de Monsieur Séguin: allusion to a *conte* by Alphonse Daudet

59   sœurs latines : nations with a language and culture derived from Latin

Possible comparisons: Vb, 16, 66, 71, 75, 76

Robert Desnos, 1900–1945

Couplets de la rue Saint-Martin

Je n'aime plus la rue Saint-Martin
Depuis qu'André Platard l'a quittée.
Je n'aime plus la rue Saint-Martin
Je n'aime rien, pas même le vin.

5   Je n'aime plus la rue Saint-Martin
Depuis qu'André Platard l'a quittée
C'est mon ami, c'est mon copain.
Nous partagions la chambre et le pain.
Je n'aime plus la rue Saint-Martin.

10   C'est mon ami, c'est mon copain.
Il a disparu un matin,
Ils l'ont emmené, on ne sait plus rien.
On ne l'a plus revu dans la rue Saint-Martin.

Pas la peine d'implorer les saints,
15   Saints Merri, Jacques, Gervais et Martin,
Pas même Valérien qui se cache sur sa colline.
Le temps passe, on ne sait rien.
André Platard a quitté la rue Saint Martin.

1942
(*Destinée arbitraire*)
©Editions Gallimard

Possible comparisons: 25, 35

75

Raymond Queneau, 1903–1976

Pour un Art Poétique

Bon dieu de bon dieu que j'ai envie d'écrire un petit poème
Tiens en voilà justement un qui passe
Petit petit petit
viens ici que je t'enfile
5   sur le fil du collier de mes autres poèmes
viens ici que je t'entube
dans le comprimé de mes œuvres complètes
viens ici que je t'empapouète
et que je t'enrime
10   et que je t'enrythme
et que je t'enlyre
et que je t'enpégase
et que je t'enverse
et que je t'enprose

15   la vache
il a foutu le camp

(Bucoliques)
©Editions Gallimard

8   empapouète : a distortion of the slang word *empapaouter* or *empapahuter', 'to sodomise'*. In the context of the sequence of (mostly invented) verbs denoting the poet's treatment of a prospective poem, it may be a fanciful contamination with *papou (Papuan* – people or language). *Enfile* and *entube* have similar obscene meanings.

Possible comparisons: 23, 52, 57, 62, 73

Raymond Queneau, 1903–1976

Le Voyageur et son ombre

Un voyageur pensif en fronçant fort son front
contemplait la nature énorme énorme chose
pleine de mystères et de contradictions
pleine de boules puantes et de fleurs écloses
5   Tout autour s'étendaient les prés et la verdure
les volcans les jardins les rochers et l'azur
les forêts les radis les oiseaux les pinsons
les golfes les déserts les bœufs les charançons
et le penseur pensif toujours fronçant sa hure
10   contemplait contemplait contemplait la nature
Il se mit à pleuvoir Alors le voyageur
ouvrit son parapluie et regarda quelle heure
il était à sa montre et reprit son chemin
en murmurant tout bas : moi je n'y comprends rien

(*Battre la campagne*)
©Editions Gallimard

8   boules puantes: *attrape répandant une odeur infecte* (Larousse)

Possible comparisons: VIa, 13, 15, 17, 21, 23, 25

René Char, 1907–1988

La Chambre dans l'espace

Tel le chant du ramier quand l'averse est prochaine – l'air se poudre de pluie, de soleil revenant –, je m'éveille lavé, je fonds en m'élevant; je vendange le ciel novice.

Allongé contre toi, je meus ta liberté. Je suis un bloc de terre
5 qui réclame sa fleur.

Est-il gorge menuisée plus radieuse que la tienne? Demander c'est mourir!

L'aile de ton soupir met un duvet aux feuilles. Le trait de mon amour ferme ton fruit, le boit.

10 Je suis dans la grâce de ton visage que mes ténèbres couvrent de joie.

Comme il est beau ton cri qui me donne ton silence!

(*Les Matinaux*)
© Editions Gallimard

Possible comparisons: 21, 58, 79, 81

Julien Gracq, 1910-

Le vent froid de la nuit

Je l'attendais le soir dans le pavillon de chasse, près de la
Rivière Morte. Les sapins dans le vent hasardeux de la nuit
secouaient des froissements de suaire et des craquements
d'incendie. La nuit noire était doublée de gel, comme le
5   satin blanc sous un habit de soirée, – au-dehors, des mains
frisées couraient de toutes parts sur la neige. Les murs étaient
de grands rideaux sombres, et sur les steppes de neige des
nappes blanches, à perte de vue, comme des feux se décollent
des étangs gelés, se levait la lumière mystique des bougies.
10   J'étais le roi d'un peuple de forêts bleues, comme un pèlerinage
avec ses bannières se range immobile sur les bords d'un lac de
glace. Au plafond de la caverne bougeait par instants, immobile
comme la moire d'une étoffe, le cyclone des pensées noires.
15   En habit de soirée, accoudé à la cheminée et maniant un
revolver dans un geste de théâtre, j'interrogeais par
désœuvrement l'eau verte et dormante de ces glaces très
anciennes; une rafale plus forte parfois l'embuait d'une sueur
fine comme celle des carafes, mais j'émergeais de nouveau,
20   spectral et fixe, comme un marié sur la plaque de photographe
qui se dégage des remous de plantes vertes. Ah! les heures
creuses de la nuit, pareilles à un qui voyage sur les os légers et
pneumatiques d'un rapide – mais soudain elle était là, assise
toute droite dans ses longues étoffes blanches.

(*Liberté grande*)
©Librairie José Corti

Possible comparisons: IV, 63, 70

Léo Ferré, 1916–

Le Lit

Cette antichambre du tombeau
Où froissent comme des drapeaux
Les draps glacés par la tempête
Ce tabernacle du plaisir
5   Avec la porte du désir
Battant sur l'ennui de la fête
Cette horizontale façon
De mettre le cœur à raison
Et le reste dans l'habitude
10   Et cette pâleur qu'on lui doit
Dès qu'on emmêle nos doigts
Pour la dernière solitude

Le lit
Fait de toile ou de plume
15   Le lit
Quand le rêve s'allume

Cette maison du rêve clos
Dans le grabat dans le berceau
Au point du jour ou de venise
20   Cette fraternité de nuit
Qui peut assembler dans un lit
L'intelligence et la bêtise
Qu'il soit de paille ou bien de soie
Pour le soldat ou pour le roi
25   Pour la putain ou la misère
Qu'il soit carré qu'il soit défait
Qu'importe lorsque l'on y fait
Autre chose que la prière

Le lit
30   Enfer pavé de roses
Le lit
Quand la mort se repose

Qu'il soit de marbre ou de sapin
Quant au lit qui sera le mien
35   Dans le néant ou la lumière
Je veux qu'on ne le fasse point
Et qu'on y laisse un petit coin

Pour un ami que j'ai sur terre
Cet ami que je laisserai
40   Quand il me faudra dételer
Pour l'aventure ou la poussière
Ce frère de mes longues nuits
Et que l'on appelle l'ennui
Au fond du lit des solitaires
45   Le lit
Quand s'endort le mystère
Sans bruit
Dans la vie passagère

(*Testament phonographe*)
©Léo Ferré

19   point de Venise: a kind of lace

Possible comparisons: I, VIa, 24, 67, 77

Georges Brassens, 1920-1981

Les Amours d'antan

Moi mes amours d'antan c'était de la grisette
Margot la blanchecaille et Fanchon la cousette
Pas la moindre noblesse excusez-moi du peu
C'étaient me direz-vous des grâces roturières
Des nymphes de ruisseau des Vénus de barrière
6   Mon prince on a les dam's du temps jadis qu'on peut

Car le cœur à vingt ans se pose où l'œil se pose
Le premier cotillon venu vous en impose
La plus humble bergère est un morceau de roi
Ça manquait de marquise on connut la soubrette
Faute de fleur de lis on eut la pâquerette
12   Au printemps Cupidon fait flèche de tout bois

On rencontrait la belle aux puces le dimanche
Je te plais tu me plais et c'était dans la manche
Et les grands sentiments n'étaient pas de rigueur
Je te plais tu me plais viens donc beau militaire
Dans un train de banlieue on partait pour Cythère
18   On n'était pas tenu mêm' d'apporter son cœur

Mimi de prime abord payait guère de mine
Chez son fourreur sans doute on ignorait l'hermine
Son habit sortait point de l'atelier d'un Dieu
Mais quand par-dessus le moulin de la Galette
Elle jetait pour vous sa parure simplette
24   C'est Psyché toute entièr' qui vous sautait aux yeux

Au second rendez-vous y avait parfois personne
Elle avait fait faux bond la petite amazone
Mais on ne courait pas se pendre pour autant
La marguerite commencée avec Suzette
On finissait de l'effeuiller avec Lisette
30   Et l'amour y trouvait quand même son content

C'était me direz-vous des grâces roturières
Des nymphes de ruisseau des Vénus de barrière
Mais c'étaient mes amours excusez-moi du peu
Des Manon des Nini des Suzon des Musette
Margot la blanchecaille et Fanchon la cousette
36   Mon prince on a les dam's du temps jadis qu'on peut.

2	blanchecaille: slang word for a laundress
12	fait flèche de tout bois : provincial expression, 'all is grist to his mill'
22	le moulin de la Galette: the famous cabaret in Montmartre, a district which retains its role as a symbol of rustic seduction, originating from the time when it lay outside the city of Paris.
24	allusion to the legend of Psyche; but the line is also an echo of Racine's *Phèdre, v.306: C'est Vénus toute entière à sa proie attachée*

Possible comparisons: 1, 14, 15, 20, 60, 67

Yves Bonnefoy, 1923-

'Ici, toujours ici'

Ici, dans le lieu clair. Ce n'est plus l'aube,
C'est déjà là, la journée aux dicibles désirs.
Des mirages d'un chant dans ton rêve il ne reste
4   Que ce scintillement de pierres à venir.

Ici, et jusqu'au soir. La rose d'ombres
Tournera sur les murs. La rose d'heures
Défleurira sans bruit. Les dalles claires
8   Mèneront à leur gré ces pas épris du jour.

Ici, toujours ici. Pierres sur pierres
Ont bâti le pays dit par le souvenir.
A peine si le bruit de fruits simples qui tombent
12   Enfièvre encore en toi le temps qui va guérir.

(Poèmes)
©Mercure de France

Possible comparisons: 33, 54, 77

Léopold Sédar Senghor, 1906–

Prière aux masques

Masques! O Masques!
Masque noir masque rouge, vous masques blanc-et-noir
Masques aux quatre points d'où souffle l'Esprit
Je vous salue dans le silence!
5   Et pas toi le dernier, Ancêtre à tête de lion
Vous gardez ce lieu forclos à tout rire de femme, à tout sourire qui se fane
Vous distillez cet air d'éternité où je respire l'air de mes Pères.
Masques aux visages sans masque, dépouillés de toute fossette comme de toute ride
Qui avez composé ce portrait, ce visage mien penché sur l'autel de papier blanc
10   A votre image, écoutez-moi!
Voici que meurt l'Afrique des empires – c'est l'agonie d'une princesse pitoyable
Et aussi l'Europe à qui nous sommes liés par le nombril.
Fixez vos yeux immuables sur vos enfants que l'on commande
Qui donnent leur vie comme le pauvre son dernier vêtement.
15   Que nous répondions présents à la renaissance du Monde
Ainsi le levain qui est nécessaire à la farine blanche.
Car qui apprendrait le rythme au monde défunt des machines et des canons?
Qui pousserait le cri de joie pour réveiller morts et orphelins à l'aurore?
Dites, qui rendrait la mémoire de vie à l'homme aux espoirs éventrés?
20   Ils nous disent les hommes du coton du café de l'huile
Ils nous disent les hommes de la mort.
Nous sommes les hommes de la danse, dont les pieds reprennent vigueur en frappant le sol dur.

(*Chants d'ombre*)
ⓒEditions du Seuil

Possible comparisons: 55, 57, 62, 83

Tchicaya U'Tamsi, 1931–1988

'Le vin pèse'

Le vin pèse sur mon cœur je souffre de jouir
Christ je hais tes chrétiens

Je suis vide d'amour pour aimer tous les lâches
Je crache sur ta joie
5   d'avoir à droite à gauche
les femmes des bourgeois
j'ai mal d'avoir bu
Ton temple a des marchands qui vendent ta croix Christ
Je vends ma négritude
10   cents sous le quatrain
Et vogue ta galère
pour des Indes soldées

Ah quel continent n'a pas ses faux nègres
j'en ai à vendre
15   Même Afrique a aussi les siens
Le Congo à ses faux nègres

Si chrétiens, seraient-ils moins sujets à caution
O je meurs à ta gloire
car tu m'as tenté
20   de m'avoir fait si triste

(*Epitomé*)
©Société Nationale d'Edition
et de Diffusion, Alger

Possible comparisons: 24, 47, 56, 82

Index of Poets

Index of Titles

Index of First Lines